e-Procurement

From Strategy to Implementation

ISBN 0-13-091411-8

90000

9 780130 914118

e-Procurement

From Strategy to Implementation

Dale Neef

FINANCIAL TIMES
Prentice Hall

Prentice Hall PTR
One Lake Street
Upper Saddle River, NJ 07458
www.phptr.com

Library of Congress Cataloging-in-Publication Data

CIP data available

Editorial/Production Supervision: PATTI GUERRIERI
Acquisitions Editor: TIM MOORE
Development Editor: RUSS HALL
Marketing Manager: TC LESZCZYNSKI
Manufacturing Buyer: MAURA ZALDIVAR
Editorial Assistant: ALLYSON KLOSS
Cover Design Director: JERRY VOTTA
Cover Design: NINA SCUDERI
Interior Design: WEE DESIGN GROUP

©2001 by Prentice Hall PTR
Prentice-Hall, Inc.
Upper Saddle River, NJ 07458

Prentice Hall books are widely used by corporations and government agencies for training, marketing, and resale.

The publisher offers discounts on this book when ordered in bulk quantities. For more information, contract: Corporate Sales Department, Phone: 800-382-3419; Fax: 201-236-7141; E-mail: corpsales@prenhall.com; or write: Prentice Hall PTR, Corp. Sales Dept. One Lake Street, Upper Saddle River, NJ 07458

Printed in the United States of America

10 9 8 7 6 5 4 3 2 1

ISBN 0-13-091411-8

Prentice-Hall International (UK) Limited, *London*
Prentice-Hall of Australia Pty. Limited, *Sydney*
Prentice-Hall Canada Inc., *Toronto*
Prentice-Hall Hispanoamericana, *S.A., Mexico*
Prentice-Hall of India Private Limited, *New Delhi*
Prentice-Hall of Japan, Inc., *Tokyo*
Pearson Education Asia Pte. Ltd.
Editora Prentice-Hall do Brasil, Ltda., *Rio de Janeiro*

FINANCIAL TIMES PRENTICE HALL BOOKS

James W. Cortada
*21st Century Business: Managing and Working
in the New Digital Economy*

Aswath Damodaran
*The Dark Side of Valuation: Valuing Old Tech, New Tech,
and New Economy Companies*

Deirdre Breakenridge
Cyberbranding: Brand Building in the Digital Economy

Dale Neef
E-procurement: From Strategy to Implementation

John R. Nofsinger
*Investment Madness: How Psychology Affects Your Investing...
And What to Do About It*

TABLE OF CONTENTS

Business people these days are becoming weary of new fads, movements, and revolutions, and rightly so. We have, in less than a decade, been taken through such "revolutionary" transformations as total quality management, business process reengineering, enterprise resource planning, activity-based costing, and retail e-commerce. Companies have downsized, outsourced, empowered employees, shifted processes and organizational structures from vertical to horizontal, completed strategic sourcing initiatives, and purchased IT systems (often on the basis of dubious return on investment), with investments amounting to millions of dollars. And, of course, they have paid management consultants and software companies many millions more for advice on implementation and change management.

Yet, completing business-to-business transactions over the Internet is genuinely something very different. The unexpected emergence of the Internet as a tool for business has meant that we have once again been thrown inescapably into the fray of major investment and change. As I have argued before[1] it is all part of an accelerated pace of change that will bring about a fundamental restructuring for all industries, worldwide, and participation is essential for the survival in the new economy.

I have written this book about e-procurement in part because I believe that there has been a mistaken emphasis on e-commerce (electronic retailing) in our approach to the use of the Internet. Swayed by the activity around online retailing—the fortunes to be made with dotcom startups, the venture capital that was available, the relative ease in which a Web site for retail sales could be built, the massive coverage of the subject by the business press—we have failed to understand that e-commerce is a relatively unimportant step in the development of the Internet. It is a vital part of an overall e-business strategy, of course, but online retailing—unless it is fully integrated into the supply chain—is simply a mildly effective extension of the sales process. Moreover, expanding revenues, given the margins made in most industries, is far less effective as a strategy than is fundamentally and permanently reducing major costs—something that affects the bottom line directly.

The real value of the Internet, as many companies are beginning to experience first hand, comes instead from business-to-business, buyer-vendor transactions that include electronic procurement and full integration of the electronic supply chain from customer to supplier. In fact, as electronic procurement and supply chain software continue to evolve, the relative value to companies of online retailing will almost certainly continue to shrink in relation to the enormous cost savings and fundamental restructuring of companies that will come about as a result of the evolution of Internet-based business-to-business activity.

The purpose of this book is threefold. First, it is simply to explain to those who have not previously dealt with the area of procurement the fundamentals involved with purchasing and replenishing materials. Though certainly not as glamorous as many (in fact, most) areas of business, procurement—whether for everyday office supplies or for materials used directly in the manufacturing process—is nonetheless an enormous expense for companies, large and small, and in every industry. In fact, so enormous is the expense and potential savings that e-procurement should from this time forward be seen as an integral part of your company's overall e-business strategy. I hope that the book can therefore serve as a primer for introducing the importance of the subject to organizational leaders and for elevating the subject from the tactical to the strategic.

The second purpose of this book is to explore the phenomenon of the electronic trading communities—the volatile and fast-growing area of online e-markets, auctions, reverse auctions, and exchanges—that is effectively revolutionizing the relationship between buyers and sellers in virtually every industry, worldwide. A battle for control over the influence and utility of these online exchanges is now being waged between a powerful group of software companies, industry-leading alliances, and third-party application service providers in a volatile mix of competition and collaboration that is at once both explosive and effective, and that will eventually affect virtually every supplier and buyer in the economy.

And finally, this book is intended to help managers, executives, and other organizational leaders to take the first important steps necessary for defining and implementing their e-procurement and overall e-business strategies. I have therefore devoted several chapters to the development of strategy, to project approach and structure, and to the activities necessary to creating an effective plan of change management. As many have learned from past lessons with enterprise resource planning systems, business benefits come not only from the functionality of the software system, but often more importantly, from changes in the way employees do their work. Just as e-procurement should be seen as strategic rather than tactical, we should also avoid seeing it solely as a technical solution. After all, to be effective, the behavior of employees in the purchasing department (not to mention the behavior of those employees throughout the organization who today buy "off contract" with little concern for price or administrative overhead costs) will need to change dramatically. For this reason, I have dedicated several chapters specifically to "lessons learned" around project and change management, relating at a more detailed level some of the leading techniques that have worked well for successful companies and consultancies in the recent past. I hope these will be useful to the soon-to-be managers of enterprise-wide e-procurement initiatives.

I should, at the outset, admit that although the book examines the basic software platforms and major players in the e-procurement industry, the business-to-business e-procurement marketplace is extremely volatile. Software vendors merge, realign, and bring forward new offerings on an almost continuous basis. Electronic markets and auction sites are multiplying rapidly, while at the same time beginning to falter and collapse, as competitors vie for dominance. The models for e-procurement—enterprise-based, outsourced, or networked—are all in a state of evolution.

In short, it is a marketplace that is constantly changing and evolving, and therefore this book is by no means the last word on the subject. But the fundamental principles behind electronic procurement are sound and well understood, and it is critical for organizational leaders to understand these principles, the major players, the marketplace, and the key issues in order to be in a position to create an e-procurement strategy with confidence. E-procurement initiatives are seldom simple, compared with building a Web page, but their potential for cost savings are enormous, and few companies have the luxury of waiting for a much more settled marketplace before acting.

ENDNOTE

1. Neef, Dale, *A Little Knowledge is a Dangerous Thing* (Butterworth-Heinemann, 1998) and *The Knowledge Economy* (Butterworth-Heinemann, 1997).

e-Procurement

From Strategy to Implementation

1

The New World of Business-to-Business E-Commerce

Objective

Business-to-business (B2B) e-commerce—the area that encompasses electronic buying and selling transactions between organizations and in which e-procurement is a central function—has become central to doing business effectively. Done well, it can help your company achieve enormous cost savings and productivity improvements.

■ B2B e-commerce has replaced business-to-consumer e-commerce as the fastest growing area of e-business in the economy.

■ E-procurement is the most important area of development in the B2B e-commerce arena.

■ E-procurement will fundamentally restructure the way in which an organization purchases goods.

■ E-procurement is coming, but for most companies their online procurement capabilities are still limited to occasional and uncoordinated shopping online for office materials.

In the future, our grand-children may ask us to tell them what life was like before the Internet in the same way we marvel at how our grand-parents managed before elec-tricity or television. Yet today, it is not obvious that the impact of the Internet has been as revolutionary as we

Nearly 80% of organizations that have rushed to establish Web sites for online retailing have failed to invest in the purchasing and distribution systems that make delivery of their products possible.

have been lead to believe. This is, in part, simply because e-commerce—online retailing—has proven to be less dra-matic in its effect on company sales, or on our everyday lives, than predicted. In fact, as we now realize, there were many mistakes made in the frenzied dotcom era that is now drawing to a close, for which many start-ups (and the con-sultancies and venture capitalists that supported them) are today paying the price. But among those errors, the worst mistake that industry generally has made is that in our enthusiasm for Web pages and online retail sales, we have ignored the far more revolutionary aspect of the Internet—business-to-business e-procurement.

It is true, electronic procurement may seem less glamor-ous and, in many ways, more difficult to initiate, than online retailing. But, in fact, e-procurement (business-to-business electronic trade) has a far greater potential for cost savings and business improvement than online retailing or enter-prise resource planning systems, and will permanently and fundamentally reform the way we do business in the future.

There is no doubt that e-commerce has been a boon to the stock exchange and has attracted vast amounts of venture capital, enormously boosting the earnings of advertising agencies, newspapers and billboards, executive recruiters, and, temporarily, at least, consultants. But as the bubble burst, it became apparent that the one group that had not benefited were the employees and investors in the dotcom companies themselves, which are, at the time of press, in virtual free fall.

In fact, a recent study by British Telecom reveals that nearly 80% of organizations that have rushed to establish Web sites for online buying have failed to invest in the purchasing and distribution systems that make delivery of the products possible. Instead of focusing on using the new Web-based technologies to streamline their supply chain, senior management of companies have focused on providing Web sites that promise much, but far too often, can deliver very little. This myopic focus on Web sites and e-commerce meant that many of the dotcom firms never came near profitability. Etoys, for example, lost more than $4 on every order. Other online start ups suffered even more. Drugstore.com lost over $16 on each non-prescription item they delivered.[1]

The entire online buying phenomenon has certainly succeeded in raising our expectations as customers to a level of near-instant gratification, with demands for ever-wider availability of goods, delivered cheaper and faster than ever before. But this combination of ever-greater expectation and consistently disappointing results—who does not have a story about the flowers that were never delivered to their mother-in-law, the books that arrived six weeks late, or the lamp shade that was left in a package on the front steps in the rain—has left many customers (and increasingly, investors) skeptical about the hyperbole of the press and the true value of online retailing.

But in many ways and for some time—at least, from an economic point of view—we have realized that providing a way for the public to buy items online was little more than an electronic extension of the sales process. There is nothing more revolutionary, once we stop for a moment and reflect, about ordering a book or flowers online than there is about ordering them over the telephone. Although having access to brochures online is convenient, and being able to send family photos electronically to friends is fun, many would argue that e-commerce has actually done little to change the nature—or more importantly, to improve the profitability—of the vast majority of "bricks and mortar" organizations.

However, just as enthusiasm for huge investments in e-commerce is beginning to wane, interest in a new area of e-business is beginning to grow. Business-to-business (B2B) e-commerce—the area which encompasses any electronic transaction between organizations and in which *e-procurement* is a central function—is set to become a major area of interest for all types of organizations. Already, B2B e-commerce accounts for more than ten times the dollars spent in consumer-based e-commerce, and even more than retail e-commerce, B2B is being touted as likely to produce enormous cost savings and productivity improvements for organizations and for the economy as a whole.

IS IT FOR REAL?

What is the scope and impact of this B2B revolution? Is it for real, or is it just more of the hyperbole that we have been witnessing with e-commerce over the past two years?

Just as with e-commerce, estimates on the effect of B2B vary widely. Gartner Group forecasts that global B2B e-commerce will reach $4 trillion by 2003—this, compared with less than $400 billion in business-to-consumer (B2C) e-commerce online sales[2] (see Figure 1.1). Similarly, AMR points out that the manufacturing sector accounted for $96 billion of Internet-based commerce in the U.S. in 1999, and this should grow at an annual rate of 78% to reach $1,700 billion by 2004.[3] Goldman Sachs predicts that B2B e-commerce will grow in the U.S. from $39 billion in 1998 to $1,500 billion in 2004 (out of a global total of $3,200 billion), at an annual growth rate of nearly 84%.[4]

For most of us, these are simply large numbers that tell us very little. But there are other, more meaningful ways of assessing the potential impact of e-procurement. A recent study by Goldman Sachs estimates that online purchasing could save firms varying

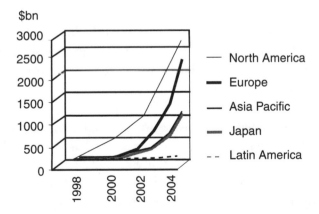

Figure 1.1 B2B E-commerce forecast by region. (Source: The Gartner Group from "Competition Rules Apply," *The Financial Times.*)

amounts, from a mere 2% on procurement costs in the mining industry to up to 40% in areas such as high-tech manufacturing and electronic components. In a study boldly entitled "The Shocking Economic Effect of B2B," the authors of the Sachs study assert that the relative effect of B2B commerce on advanced economies will far outstrip the meager efficiency advances provided by IT systems to date. B2B e-commerce "is probably," they conclude, "the single biggest macroeconomic shock to hit the world in the last 40 years or so."[5]

That may be overstating the case a bit, but in fact their estimates do seem shocking, with B2B e-commerce predicted to boost the level of productivity in the rich national economies by an average of 5% in the next decades—an extraordinary addition to the national GDP growth rate of .05% per year.[6]

The Goldman Sachs study estimates that European nations, Britain, and Japan stand to see similar productivity gains through the adoption of online purchasing. In Britain, the market for office equipment alone is estimated to be around $33 billion. In fact, if just small and medium-sized companies alone in Britain were to use the Internet to buy indirect materials, it is estimated that the savings would total some $36 billion a year, with an overall yearly productivity boost of nearly 2% of GDP.[7] As *The Economist* points out, "If the rewards from IT are significant in America, the gains in Europe, Japan, and many emerging economies could be even bigger. If so, this could yet prove to be the biggest technological revolution ever for the world as a whole."[8]

AMR Research has made similar studies and reached similar (even though couched in less apocalyptic language) conclusions. They predict that B2B e-commerce in the U.S. alone will reach some $5.7 trillion in the next three years, which, if true, would account for nearly 29% of all commercial transactions. They estimate that as software offerings mature and companies of every type move toward purchasing indirect goods—office supplies, janitorial services, and so on— online, most companies adopting e-procurement will be able to assume at least an 8% reduction in the cost of purchasing, saving U.S. companies some $82 billion by 2004. Once manufacturing and distribution companies begin adopting e-procurement systems and processes for their direct materials—those materials involved in the manufacturing process itself—the benefits to companies and the economy leap enormously, to an estimated savings of $229 billion.[9]

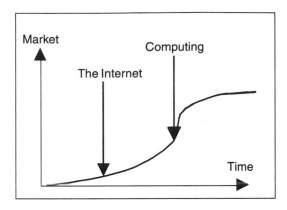

Figure 1.2 The technology curve. (Source: "The New Economy Survey," *The Economist*.)

What is more, in order to keep this potential growth in perspective, it is important to reflect that we are only at the beginning of the Internet revolution, and some industry watchers would suggest that the economy has not yet had time to begin to adjust to the revolutionary nature of Internet-based business. After all, although it may seem that we have been living with the Internet for decades, the World Wide Web is only ten years old, and browser technology before 1995 was rudimentary. Despite talk of global supply chains, only 6% of the world is online today, and although many estimates set the number of users worldwide at over a billion in the next four years, as yet, there are only some 350 million people online worldwide.

There is no doubt a good deal of truth to the assertion that B2B e-commerce is still highly immature. Economists are quick to point out that technologies like the Internet are really only at the beginning of their development (see Figure 1.2), where growth is actually relatively slow by comparison with computing or other more mature technologies generally. But just as with these other technologies, once accepted and broadly adopted, their usage will expand exponentially.

And as you will see later in this chapter, the potential of B2B is only now being recognized by a few large and fairly sophisticated firms. The promise is all in the future.

THE UNIQUE NATURE OF B2B E-PROCUREMENT

So, what is it about the nature of B2B e-commerce that gives rise to this magnitude of change and savings? The answer seems to be that, unlike online e-commerce sales that may or may not expand revenues, *B2B e-commerce will fundamentally restructure the way in which an organization purchases goods, resulting in significant process efficiencies and permanently lower costs.* Organizations are finding that the more they can integrate e-procurement processes and systems directly into their supply chain, the greater the effect in terms of cost savings and process improvement. Those improvements come about in several broad areas.

First, online procurement significantly reduces the day-to-day cost of purchasing. Electronic procurement of goods is not only far less expensive but far more efficient than the current manual, labor-intensive phone and fax-based purchasing process. Research indicates that 40% of the total cost of purchasing materials comes from transaction costs associated with processing and managing the order.[10] Not only is it faster and cheaper, but online procurement promises to reduce invoicing and ordering errors, on average, by up to 2%. This can all add up to considerable savings when these total transaction costs are taken into account. For those (at this point, usually large and albeit sophisticated companies) that have successfully adopted e-procurement, it is not unusual to see process cost reductions of up to 90%, with additional reductions in price (through contract buying and via e-exchanges) of up to 11% for the direct costs of all goods and services that they buy.[11]

3M provides a good example. Traditionally, the company has created hundreds of thousands of purchase orders for everyday office materials at an average cost of some $120 each. These orders accounted for some 70% of the volume of the company's total purchasing transactions (and, therefore, effort), and yet amounted to only 2% of the total purchasing dollars spent. Each requisition took from one to three days to process, and nearly a third of all orders required rework. Even then, an estimated 45% of purchases were made in violation of prearranged contracts with the vendors.

Over the past two years, 3M has implemented an e-procurement solution that has greatly reduced these transaction costs, almost entirely eliminating rework and errors, and has cut the internal order cycle time, including approval, to less than an hour. They estimate that the improvements will drop the average cost per purchase from $120 to $40.[12] It is a good, but not unusual, example of the magnitude of savings to be made.

A second key area of potentially revolutionary improvement can be seen in the rapid development of online electronic auctions and e-marketplaces. These provide an electronic forum in which a large numbers of buyers and sellers can meet and exchange information and bids online, greatly expanding sales opportunities for sellers, and often greatly reducing the purchase price for buyers of bulk or difficult-to-find items. There are additional benefits for small and middle-size firms—which normally lack buying power by themselves—in that the marketplace intermediaries essentially negotiate discounts on their collective behalf, creating economies of scale normally reserved for large and powerful firms.

These electronic marketplaces have developed explosively since 1999, and there are now more than 1,000 (serving as an electronic exchange for everything from wine to bananas, steel to chemicals, automobiles to aerospace) in the U.S. and more than 250 in Europe. In fact, research carried out by Deloitte Consulting in July 2000 identified 1,447 separate electronic marketplaces that had been either launched or announced, and at least in the short term, these numbers will continue to grow. If they continue at their present growth rate, Net Market Makers estimates that there will be as many as 20,000 by 2003.

Although most analysts agree that there will be a severe "shake out" of exchanges through mergers, acquisitions, and failures in the next several months (Deloitte predicts no more than 400 e-marketplaces will still be trading in four years' time), the development of these electronic markets promises to revolutionize the way companies purchase materials worldwide.[13]

One of the most important and economically curious developments in this area, has been the collaboration of large and powerful industry leaders working together to sponsor vertical industry e-marketplaces and trading communities. Known as *market creators,* these collaborative exchanges are backed by levels of industry knowledge and financial clout that promise to drive their supplier networks quickly toward adopting e-procurement policies. One highly publicized example is Covisint, a joint electronic exchange being sponsored by GM, Ford, Daimler Chrysler, and Renault-Nissan, with a turnover of $250 billion and 60,000 suppliers. Major tier-one vendors, such as Dana Corporation, one of the world's largest suppliers of parts for automobile manufacturers, have already agreed to participate, hoping that the Covisint exchange will provide them with a primary link directly into the supply chain of major auto manufacturers. Covisint estimates that once all of their suppliers are connected online, they can achieve cost reductions of up to 14% on the production of the average car.

Again, the advantages accrue from a combination of greater efficiencies and lower negotiated prices. And the important thing to note—at least from an economic point of view—is that while price reductions simply shift money between buyers and sellers, greater efficiencies create a permanent gain in productivity, and therefore profit, for both parties and the for the economy as a whole.

Finally, and possibly most importantly, online procurement—and eventually totally electronic materials management—can completely revolutionize a manufacturing or distribution firm's supply chain, making a seamless flow of order fulfillment information from customer to supplier (see Figure 1.3). This was something that was inconceivable just a few years ago when Enterprise Resource Planning (ERP), Customer Relationship Management (CRM), and supply chain systems remained physically and logically separated and piecemeal. *It was only with the shift from client-server to Web-based technologies that a true consolidation of data—a single, extended enterprise-system approach—became possible.*

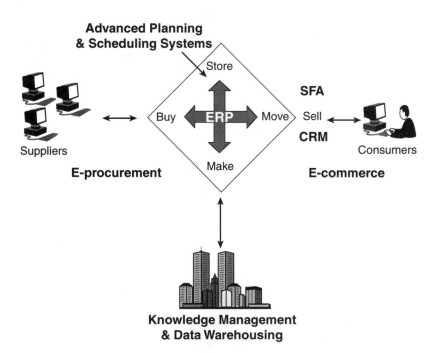

Figure 1.3 Components of collaborative fulfillment and an integrated e-business strategy.

This can greatly improve efficiency in several obvious ways. First, better information concerning customer demand means that firms can move much closer to the ideal of Just-In-Time (JIT) manufacturing and greatly reduce the amount of excessive inventories and expensive safety stock. Electronic replenishment also eliminates the multiple, inefficient layers within a firm's supply chain. Not only does a fully-integrated online supply chain system allow firms to purchase goods from their vendors easily and accurately, on pre-agreed terms, but it provides them with opportunities to communicate changes in design and manufacturing requirements quickly along the full length of the supply chain, through multiple levels of suppliers.

All of this means that for the first time in history, a manufacturing firm can truly incorporate JIT manufacturing techniques, eliminating safety stock, excess carrying costs, and production of unwanted goods. Bringing transparency and continuity to that extended supply chain means that firms can edge much closer to achieving what Dell's CFO Tom Meredith suggested nearly three years ago—that "when the customer clicks the mouse, our suppliers will feel the ping."[14]

This level of collaborative fulfillment—the seamless integration of software and process that allows for complete visibility of the real-time order fulfillment process to all partners—is of course a distant ideal for most manufacturing firms. And yet many progressive companies are even now moving closer to an "available to promise" electronic process that will eventually mean they achieve the nirvana of manufacturing gurus—the "sell one/make one" supply chain.

DRAGGING THEIR FEET

If all of this is going to happen, however, it certainly hasn't happened yet. Although the few that have made the investment—companies like Federal Express, Chevron, United Technologies, Microsoft, British Telecom, and Texas Instruments—are reaping significant returns, they tend to be the exception rather than the rule. These organizations tend to be culturally progressive industry leaders with strengths in high technology and leading-edge processes. When combined with enormous purchasing budgets, they have found the potential returns on investment from e-procurement to be too compelling to ignore.

Despite the persuasive statistics and the significant returns by the early industry leaders, most companies are at best only in the early planning stages of their e-procurement strategies. Part of the problem is simply that for most companies the procurement process is still seen as tactical rather than strategic—as a cost rather than a benefit—to the company. In fact, a recent survey by Deloitte indicated that despite the fact that some 90% of businesses interviewed claimed that e-procurement is "part of their ongoing business plan," very few companies have any broad strategy for e-procurement that involves their supply chain, and incredibly, only 1% of respondents to a 1999 survey by W.W. Grainger said they used an Internet-based software platform to purchase office materials. Similar bad news from the suppliers' side—PriceWaterhouseCoopers found that while almost every company interviewed recognized the importance of business-to-business transactions, more than 25% said that they had no functionality beyond basic online "brochureware."[15]

Unfortunately, by all indications, an e-procurement strategy for most U.S. companies is still limited to occasional and uncoordinated shopping online for office supplies. Few have associated e-procurement with the purchase of mission-critical, direct manufacturing materials, and despite investing heavily in ERP and advanced planning and scheduling platforms, most manufacturing and distribution companies still admit that their processes for managing procurement are "ill defined or not defined at all." In fact, despite years of focus on strategic sourcing and VMI (Vendor-Managed Inventory), according to W.W. Grainger, only 14% of large companies in 1999 had an integrated supply chain relationship with their vendors.[16] As might be expected, those relationships are skewed almost entirely toward their largest suppliers. The average Fortune 500 company may purchase from up to 10,000 suppliers, but are seldom connected electronically to more than a handful—25 to 50—of their largest tier-one vendors. Only one half of one percent of suppliers to the Fortune 500 companies are currently connected to e-procurement—mostly EDI (Electronic Data Interchange)—systems.[17]

Europe, for the most part, is even less well-advanced in their preparations. They began more slowly, and Web-based buying from suppliers is still in its infancy. Forrester Research claimed that in 1999, they struggled to find even 20 firms beyond an e-procurement pilot phase that could qualify as "sophisticated multinationals,"—those that had well-developed e-procurement strategies for both indirect and direct goods. They classified a further 600 companies as "aware," meaning that they had begun to make the necessary investments but were still struggling to implement solutions and get a return on investment.[18] A recent study by Net Profit in Europe found that although there was a very high level of interest in e-procurement among European companies—58% were considering an Internet-based purchasing system and 75% of respondents thought that the Internet would be "very" or "extremely" important for procurement in three years' time—only 14% of companies had actually installed systems.[19]

When it comes to integrating e-procurement into direct supply chain materials, the U.K. fared poorly. In a survey that covered both small and large-sized U.K. companies, The Chartered Institute of Purchasing and Supply found that only 23% had a comprehensive supply chain strategy, and only 17% reported viewing supply chain procurement as important enough to merit board-level representation. Only 5% of current procurement spending is completed online.[20]

There are many explanations given by company executives for this hesitancy to take the plunge into e-procurement. One obvious reason is that despite today's general atmosphere of "e-panic" in the media, a huge number of U.S. small and mid-sized companies—around 35%—still have no access to online services. For others, particularly for small and medium-sized manufacturing and distribution companies, the entire concept of e-procurement via the Internet is a fairly recent phenomenon, and they simply have had little time to come to grips with its implications.

More often, companies complain that although they have access to the Internet, there remains such a complete separation between the Internet and any of their company's legacy systems, that even when they select products from online catalogs, they are forced to work through the same old manual, paper-based requisition and purchase order process. A recent survey by W.W. Grainger revealed that more than two-thirds of respondents said they used the Internet to get product information, even though they couldn't actually order online.[21]

Other companies explain that they are not slow in realizing the potential benefits of e-procurement for both indirect and direct materials, but are simply too busy and too unfamiliar with all the options to begin the potentially enormous effort required to select, buy, and integrate systems. This is particularly frustrating for procurement officers in manufacturing and distribution companies who feel comfortable moving more rapidly into online procurement of indirect materials—maintenance and repair items, office supplies, travel services—but are held back by corporate leaders who cannot yet decide whether or not their indirect procurement strategy should be part of, or separate from, their wider supply chain procurement and replenishment strategy. And many company leaders are still justifiably concerned about the daunting prospect of integrating multiple systems—demand planning, ERP materials management, payment systems, and so on—particularly in the context of ever-changing major software platforms and e-procurement offerings.

Interestingly, probably the most often-cited reason for not moving immediately into e-procurement has been concerns over security and trust. For most companies, some of their most important assets are their buying plans, their pricing models, and their new product designs. Many executives are concerned that once information goes outside the company firewall, these key assets may be exposed to competitive eyes. In the PriceWaterhouseCoopers survey of senior business leaders in the U.K., Germany, France, and the Netherlands, these types of security issues were cited as the most important factor holding back e-procurement progress. This was particularly true in the case of online procurement of mission-critical direct materials, where issues concerning third-party security and the delivery reliability of unknown vendors made procurement officers hesitant to give up their (admittedly cumbersome) paper-based process conducted with long-time, trusted suppliers.[22]

For these and other reasons, most companies are still in the very early phases of developing and implementing their e-procurement strategy, still trying to understand their many options, weighing up the pros and cons of plunging into the fray, or holding back until more is known about this fast-changing and unpredictable area of e-business. Based on any number of recent studies, it is safe to assume that the majority of organizations—buyers and sellers—will not have a fully implemented and integrated e-procurement process in place for at least the next three years.

This hesitancy, however, does not mean that the e-procurement revolution is not going to happen. Software providers are quickly rising to the challenge, and in many ways, it is software that drives this marketplace. According to Killen & Associates, the combined software, electronic catalog services, procurement payment systems, and implementation services jumped from a mere $300 million in 1997 to nearly $725 million in 2000.[23]

Very real competitive forces are driving companies to extend and integrate their supply chain and to reduce their purchasing costs— both for indirect and for direct inventories. These forces include the enormity of potential savings, the rapid move toward agreement on standards, and the push and pull from powerful industry leaders. And, interestingly, from an economic point of view, the value to each individual participant increases as more suppliers and buyers participate in the e-procurement marketplace.

IS B2B 4 U?

Given this mixture of intense competitive pressures, a turbulent marketplace, and widespread managerial hesitancy, what is the best way to begin moving forward toward making a decision about your company's e-procurement strategy?

As always, one way is simply to look at the business case for e-procurement at an organizational level. It is worth noting that, for one thing, the return on investment for e-procurement tends to be much greater than any of the business improvement revolutions—business process reengineering, strategic sourcing, activity-based costing, ERP—that have preoccupied organizations for the past decade.

To understand why the return on investment for e-procurement can be so significant, it is first important to understand the sheer dollar magnitude of procurement-related activities in the average company. Doing this for indirect materials—office supplies, maintenance and repair parts and services, travel planning and booking, and so on—is much more straightforward, of course, than the infinitely more complex activities of the modern supply chain, which will be examined in more detail later.

There are at least two good ways to put your procurement spending in perspective. The first is simply to look at the percentage of total revenue that your company spends on non-production purchasing costs. Using this approach, the Center for Advanced Purchasing Studies estimates that the average company tends to spend 40% of its revenue on non-production purchasing, depending, of course, on the industry.[24] W.W. Grainger sets the figure slightly higher, averaging nearer 60% of total expenditures.[25] That means that for every dollar a firm earns, between 40 and 60 cents is spent on maintenance, repairs, office materials, and employee services.

Although a huge amount of money, these figures simply reflect the prices paid for goods and do not take into account the significant transaction costs associated with those purchases in terms of labor, time, and delays. *In reality, price is neither the only nor the major component of cost to an organization when estimating procurement spending.* In fact, a recent study by Group Trade concluded that although leveraging your buying power through online e-markets might reduce the price paid by 10% to 20%, the real value to the company—up to 70% of total savings—comes from savings realized through reducing transaction costs.[26]

This tends to be one of the most pressing problems with large-scale procurement, generally. The fact is, without accurate, real-time decision support tools that can help a company to understand the underlying costs of the process—transaction costs, vendor delivery or quality issues—firms (and individual departments) far too often focus exclusively on price, many times at the expense of broader "value creation" opportunities. It is usually true in any endeavor: you get what you pay for, and a focus on price alone often results in ultimately higher costs because of unpredictability or poor supplier performance. This is particularly true in maintenance and direct material purchasing situations where certainty of the right materials, delivered at the right time to the right place, can be far more valuable than a lower price per high volume or per item. Too often, companies suffer through devastating delays, shutdowns, or recall situations simply because they have bought in bulk or for price (as many manufacturers have found to their frustration with recent purchases from unknown sellers completed through online exchanges). Equally, from a supplier's perspective, adding value through quality services is much more profitable and predictable than a price race to the bottom.

More important, of course, is what level of savings organizations themselves can expect to make by eliminating slow, inaccurate, and costly paper-based processes. These savings are best measured in terms of transaction costs, which include things such as lost discounts and "maverick" buying, hours spent in supplier relationship management, time and labor hours spent in the paper-based order generation, requisitioning and approval process, quality assurance, returns, capital cost of warehouses' excess inventory, carrying costs that come as a result of disconnected replenishment channels, shop-floor downtime from items needed but missing, and so on. These are the types of savings that should be measured into the equation to get an accurate picture of the scale of improvements that can come from fully automating this procurement process.

Looking at these transaction costs themselves provides a second way of gauging relative procurement costs. Even today, the vast majority of purchasing transactions of indirect materials is done in varying combinations of telephone (still used by 85% of companies), faxed orders (used by 65% of companies), or face-to-face discussions with suppliers (50% of companies). Using these slow and labor-intensive (if personal) methods, the average transaction cost tends to be somewhere between $80 and $110 for each order. The Aberdeen Group sets average indirect transaction costs at $107 per order. British Telecom set its average pre-e-procurement transaction cost at $80.[27]

Although prices can be driven down through better vendor management, adherence to discounts, and the reduction of maverick buying, the big savings come through greatly reducing these transaction costs. To understand the scale of what automating your procurement process can do, consider data offered by those who have initiated strong e-procurement programs:

- British Telecoms claim to have cut their average transaction cost from $80 to $8 dollars on a volume of $1.3 million in transactions.[28]

- The Aberdeen Group reports that e-procurement systems have dropped the average transaction cost for the companies they surveyed from $107 to $30, with a corresponding drop in average cycle time from 7.3 days to 2 days.[29]

- IBM says that they cut the average cost of generating an order from $35 to less than a dollar.[30]

- Raytheon Systems are predicting a reduction in the cost of their purchase orders from $100 per piece to less than $3.[31]

- Microsoft reduced direct purchasing costs from $60 to $5, and claims to have reduced its purchasing department from 29 to 2 full-time purchasing employees.[32]

- Companies report reducing transaction costs by as much as 75% over traditional phone or fax-based ordering.[33]

- The *Wall Street Journal* sets the average cost of a paper-based purchase order at $150 and an e-commerce PO at $25.[34]

BANK OF IRELAND TAKES LEAD ON E-PROCUREMENT

The Bank of Ireland is a good example of the potential savings that can be made. The bank spends an average £330 million each year in purchasing ORM materials, and found that it had some 37 different standalone purchasing systems and procurement processes. Its supplier list had not been rationalized in years. Following implementation of a full e-procurement initiative— which included programs for vendor rationalization, process improvement, and systems implementation—it reported saving 30%—nearly £Ir1 million in one year.

Source: Billinge, Colin, "Everyone Needs a Leader," *The Financial Times* "Understanding E-Procurement" Survey, Winter 2000, p. 14.

These figures are especially impressive given that most e-procurement systems are still in their design infancy and involve only indirect goods. Companies have seldom integrated these systems well into their direct production purchasing processes—an area of enormous savings yet to come.

As astounding as the improvement in transaction costs appear, they are borne out by corresponding return on investment (ROI) figures. According to the Aberdeen Group, within the first full year of deployment, companies have been able to realize more than a 300 percent return on investment through Internet-based e-procurement systems.[35] A study completed by Deloitte Consulting last year found that of over 200 organizations currently involved with e-procurement projects—with average implementation costs of between $2 and $4 million— reported savings averaged 9% over the first two years.[36] A similar study by W.W. Grainger set an average ROI for buying companies installing e-procurement systems of between 245 and 400 percent. And although sellers showed much smaller returns of between 10% and 15%, through moving online, they were able to increase their sales by an average of 300%.[37]

Few businessmen can be unmoved by figures like these, and yet many believe that the most significant long-term savings will come not from greater efficiency alone, but also from freeing up procurement employees from the drudgery of day-to-day transaction processing, and refocusing their talents on strategic sourcing activities. And, because of the nature of an all-inclusive e-procurement system, one of the most important benefits to be realized with automation of the procurement process is that, for the first time, an organization will be able to accurately track costs for labor, error reconciliation, lost orders, maverick buying, and delays in the process. One of the most telling revelations coming from the myriad of studies being done on this subject is that, incredibly, very few companies can provide accurate figures for money lost through noncontract or maverick buying, or calculate with any reasonable level of accuracy the volumes of spending per vendor on contracts that might allow them to negotiate improved terms or discounts. Large companies seldom can identify their suppliers across the entire enterprise or break down with any precision the nature of their spending with key suppliers or by operating divisions.

In short, companies that have invested strongly in e-procurement have not only found a significant return on their investment, but have come a long way in being able to get an accurate grasp on where and why they spend.

Finally, whatever the exact numbers, it is worth keeping in mind that savings from procurement costs can be applied directly to the bottom line, which in effect makes them more valuable than two to three times that amount in revenue growth alone. In fact, according to some studies, a 10% reduction in procurement costs can result in up to a nearly 50% rise in profit margin.[38]

However we measure the potential savings, though, it is quickly becoming obvious that e-procurement is a viable and valuable new way of doing business, and although still in its early days, promises to be something that will soon be adopted by companies large and small. In this book, then, we work under the premise that not only can e-procurement be a valuable new opportunity for most organizations in the coming years, but that with the relentless push by software companies, powerful market creators, and government, the wide adoption of e-procurement is virtually inevitable. Accordingly, we will explore in this book the various important aspects of this new economic and business phenomenon in order to understand what it is and why it is important, and to help companies just beginning to anticipate the shift toward online purchasing to be able to move more quickly toward an e-procurement initiative—from strategy through implementation.

ENDNOTES

1. "A Virtual Investment," *The Financial Times*, December 5, 2000, p. 18.
2. "The New Economy Survey," *The Economist*, September 23, 2000, pp. 10–11.
3. Nairn, Geoffrey, "Ripples From a Quiet Revolution Bring Net Gains for Manufacturing Sector," *The Financial Times IT Survey*, November 1, 2000, pt. I.
4. Fisher, Andrew, "Many Markets Set for Macroeconomic Shock," *The Financial Times IT Review*, October 18, 2000, pt. V.
5. Brookes, Martin, "The Shocking Economic Effect of B2B," The Goldman Sachs Group, Inc., pt. V.
6. "The New Economy Survey," *The Economist*, September 23, 2000, p. 11.
7. "Could B2B B4U?", *The Economist*, May 27, 2000, p. 79.
8. "The New Economy Survey," *The Economist*, September 23, 2000, p. 7.
9. Nairn, Geoffrey, "Ripples From a Quiet Revolution Bring Net Gains for Manufacturing Sector," *The Financial Times IT Survey*, November 1, 2000, p. 1.
10. "E-Procurement: The Transformation of Corporate Purchasing," Time, Inc. in association with AMR Research, Inc., May 2, 2000, ©2001 Time Inc., all rights reserved. www.fortune.com/sections/eprocurement2000, retrieved July 19, 2000.
11. "The New Economy Survey," *The Economist*, September 23, 2000, p. 11.
12. "E-Procurement: Unleashing Corporate Purchasing Power," Time, Inc. in association with AMR Research, Inc., May 2, 2000, ©2001 Time Inc., all rights reserved. www.fortune.com/sections/eprocurement2000, retrieved July 19, 2000.
13. Newing, Rod, "Internet Rain Puts a Bloom on the Business-to-Business Marketplace," *The Financial Times IT Survey*, November 1, 2000, p. I; Brown, Malcolm, "Bluffers' Guide to B2B Marketplaces," *The Financial Times IT Survey*, November 1, 2000, pt. III, V.
14. Nairn, Geoffrey, "Ripples From a Quiet Revolution Bring Net Gains for Manufacturing Sector," *The Financial Times IT Survey*, November 1, 2000, pt. I.
15. Trommer, Diane, "Myth vs. Reality," *ZDNet: Tech InfoBase*, June 12, 2000, p. 1.

16. Gartner Group, "A CEO's Internet Business Strategy Checklist: The Leading Questions," *Business Technology Journal,* April 1999; "Survey: How Companies Order MRO Supplies," *Modern Distribution Management,* 30.04, February 25, 2000, p. 7.

17. "E-Procurement: Unleashing Corporate Purchasing Power," Time, Inc. in association with AMR Research, Inc., May 2, 2000, ©2001 Time Inc., all rights reserved. www.fortune.com/sections/eprocurement2000, retrieved July 19, 2000.

18. From The Forrester Group's report "Net Buying Benefits," as cited by Mark Vernon, "Livelier Image for a Low-Profile Task," *The Financial Times,* March 24, 1999, p. 16; Batchelor, Charles, "Logistics Aspires to Worldly Wisdom," *The Financial Times,* June 17, 1999, p. 17.

19. Bowen, David, "The Magic of Online Trading," in "Understanding E-Procurement," *The Financial Times,* Winter 2000, p. 10.

20. Batchelor, Charles, "Logistics Aspires to Worldly Wisdom," *The Financial Times,* June 17, 1999, p. 17; Ward, Hazel, "Bosses Voice E-Procurement Fears," *Computer Weekly,* July 20, 2000, p. 2.

21. "Survey: How Companies Order MRO Supplies," *Modern Distribution Management,* 30.04, February 25, 2000, p. 3.

22. Ward, Hazel, "Bosses Voice E-Procurement Fears," *Computer Weekly,* July 20, 2000, p. 2.

23. "Boost Your Purchasing Power With Web Software," www.datamation.earthweb.com/enap/01buy3.

24. Dyck, Timothy, "Big Payoffs for E-Commerce Adopters," *ZDNet: eWeek,* November 16, 1998.

25. Brack, Ken, "E-Procurement: The Next Frontier," *Industrial Distribution,* January 1, 2000, p. 3.

26. "Could B2B B4U?", *The Economist,* May 27, 2000, p. 79.

27. "Survey: How Companies Order MRO Supplies," *Modern Distribution Management,* 30.04, February 25, 2000, p. 1; Brack, Ken, "E-Procurement: The Next Frontier," *Industrial Distribution,* January 1, 2000, p. 3; "Business-to-business Sales Set to Soar," *Financial Times Survey,* October 20, 1999, p. 2.

28. "Business-to-business Sales Set to Soar," *Financial Times Survey,* October 20, 1999, p. 2.

29. Brack, Ken, "E-Procurement: The Next Frontier," *Industrial Distribution,* January 1, 2000, p. 3.

30. McDonald, Sheila, "Top Story: B2B Hits the Trenches," *ElectricNews.net,* April 28, 2000, p. 2.

31. Dyck, Timothy, "Big Payoffs for E-Commerce Adopters," *ZDNet: eWeek,* November 16, 1998.

32. Dyck, Timothy, "Big Payoffs for E-Commerce Adopters," *ZDNet: eWeek,* November 16, 1998.

33. Dyck, Timothy, "Big Payoffs for E-Commerce Adopters," *ZDNet: eWeek,* November 16, 1998.

34. "E-Procurement: The Transformation of Corporate Purchasing," Time, Inc. in association with AMR Research, Inc., May 2, 2000, ©2001 Time Inc., all rights reserved. www.fortune.com/sections/eprocurement2000, retrieved July 19, 2000.

35. "E-Procurement: Transformation of Corporate Purchasing," Time, Inc. in association with AMR Research, Inc., May 2, 2000, ©2001 Time Inc., all rights reserved. www.fortune.com/fortune/sections/eprocurement2000, retrieved July 19, 2000.

36. "Leveraging the E-Business Marketplace," Deloitte Consulting, Fall 1999, www.dc.com/services/product.asp.

37. "Study Shows Big Rewards for B2B E-Commerce Procurement," *E-Commerce Times,* part of News Factor Network (www.NewsFactor.com), October 1, 1999, p. 1.

38. Fisher, Andrew, "It's a Small World After All," in "Understanding E-Procurement," *The Financial Times,* Winter 2000, p. 6.

2

The Fundamentals of Procurement

Objective

One reason for the confusion surrounding e-procurement is that the press often lumps all procurement into a single group, as if all purchasing techniques and commodity groups required the same systems and approach. This is not so, and several key distinctions should be made when considering your company's e-procurement strategy.

■ Procurement materials can be broken down into two major categories: indirect and direct.

■ Indirect procurement involves any commodity or service that does not result directly in finished goods.

■ Indirect procurement can be divided into two groups: ORM (e.g., office products and travel services) and MRO (e.g., replacement parts) materials.

■ Direct procurement involves materials purchased for use in manufacturing or distribution that are "directly" related to the production of finished goods.

■ With e-procurement, the traditional division between direct and indirect purchasing paths is beginning to blur.

Traditionally, procurement has been broken down into two major categories: indirect and direct. In general terms, indirect procurement describes all of the day-to-day necessities of the workplace—staplers, paper, furniture, laptop computers, pencils, travel services—those things that tend to be of low value per item, but are usually bought in high volumes. In the typical company, indirect procurement accounts for 60% to 80% of all purchasing transactions.

All companies—whether manufacturing, distribution, retail, financial, or professional services—purchase large amounts of non-production, indirect goods, usually spending an eye-opening average of 40% to 60% of the total revenue of the company.

Direct Materials: those materials involved in the manufacturing supply chain that are "directly" related to the production of finished goods.

Indirect Materials: any commodity or service that a company buys that does not result directly in finished goods.

Direct materials, obviously then, are those involved in the manufacturing supply chain that are *directly* related to the production of finished goods. These materials tend to be purchased in large volumes, and depending on the level of sophistication of a company's forecasting and planning capacity, are, at least to purchasing specialists, fairly predictable in name, if not in exact amounts. Purchasing officers in aluminum manufacturing companies know they need to procure certain quantities of bauxite and aluminum at certain times during the manufacturing process. High-technology manufacturers know that they will require microchips, wiring, and other components. Procurement of direct goods, then, is of concern only to manufacturing, distribution, or retail companies—those that create, assemble, or move large numbers or amounts of finished or perishable goods. Because of their predictability and high volume, procurement of direct materials accounts for far fewer purchasing transactions (between 20% and 40% in manufacturing companies), but can account for up to 60% of a manufacturing firm's total procurement expenditure.[1]

INDIRECT PROCUREMENT: ORM VERSUS MRO

ORM (Operating Resource Management): ordinary office products and services that organizations purchase day to day.

The term ORM (Operating Resource Management) is now used commonly to describe the many ordinary office products and services that organizations purchase day to day: office supplies, furniture, forms, travel services, computers, janitorial and maintenance services, light bulbs, extension cords, and the like. Usually thought of as high-volume and low-dollar items, they nonetheless amount to a significant portion of a company's total spending. To give some idea of the scale, in the U.S. alone in 2000, the overall market for ORM products and services reached $725 million.

Over the years, the abbreviation MRO—for Maintenance, Repair and Operations—has come into popular use, and today most software vendors selling solutions for indirect materials (and, therefore, the popular business press) have begun to mistakenly lump all indirect goods together under this heading. But there is an important distinction that should be made. Office products should not be confused with mission critical overhaul or maintenance items. In purchasing, the two groups of goods are often known as *white collar ORM* (staples and notepads) and *blue collar MRO* (replacement parts), and the respective purchasing processes in terms of the levels of complexity, cost, and volume, vary enormously. Many analysts believe that MRO is in fact the much more important of the two.

"In spite of the current hype about the ability to buy office products or janitorial supplies over the Web," contends Lisa Williams of the Yankee Group, "the real 'gating' factor to growing this B2B e-commerce market will be the use of the Internet to manage and procure mission-critical items such as

MRO (Maintenance, Repair and Operations): mission critical overhaul or maintenance items.

component parts, expensive plant spares, and outsourced manufactured items."[2]

Certainly, procurement of white collar indirect supplies tends to be less complex than procurement of blue collar, or industrial, MRO, for obvious reasons. Indirect goods are seldom time or mission-critical, and as important as pencils or notepads are, items like these can be purchased from any number of wholesale—or retail—vendors, each selling similar, if not identical, brands. These items can easily be described and cataloged—black ball-point pens or bond white liquid paper—and therefore do not require the specialist expertise necessary when purchasing complex electrical repair components or highly engineered machine parts necessary for maintenance of complex manufacturing equipment. After all, it is much easier to quickly look up in a catalog—or run down to the local retail outlet—to purchase paper clips than it is to search for and procure a specially tempered, metal valve stem.

The consequences of misordering are also obviously different (see Table 2.1). Getting the wrong color ball point pen is bad, but buying the wrong shear pin or gasket for a critical assembly-line component can be catastrophic. Also blue collar MRO orders are often single-sourced, purchased in limited quantities, and are necessary to prevent the shutdown of the production lines. Blue collar MRO orders can easily amount to several hundreds of thousands of dollars, and require special service contracts. Blue collar items are often listed as inventory, tied into the company's inventory system, and accompanied with critical and complex design and performance regulations. Purchasing and maintenance employees often need to do a good deal of time-consuming prescreening of suppliers in order to understand which vendors will be trustworthy. MRO buyers are usually looking for high levels of quality control and technical support from their suppliers, so that replacement parts are delivered quickly, often at a few hours' notice. As a result, the average company uses up to 50 different MRO suppliers, and over a third of U.S. companies use 50 or more.[3]

There are two key cost areas in indirect procurement. The first is simply the straightforward inefficiency and labor-intensity of the process itself. For most companies, the centralized purchasing function has traditionally been responsible for buying a good portion of all indirect, non-production goods—whether blue or white collar—

A COMPARISON OF WHITE COLLAR ORM AND BLUE COLLAR MRO

Issues	"White Collar" ORM	"Blue Collar" MRO	TABLE 2.1
Number of Orders	Moderate	Often hundreds of thousands	
Quantity per Order	Few to moderate	Varies from one to thousands	
Delivery Criticality	Generally low	Routine to critical to the point of work stoppage for delivery failures	
Ratio of Single Source	Low	High percentage (up to 30% by count, more by value); may be singe/very limited sourced	
Services/ Contracts	Some	Almost always required—performance is critical in many cases	
Accounting Tie Back	Generally only to a GL account	May be multiple—to work order, equipment, GL and other accounts, capital tie back as well	
Controlled Inventory	Rarely	Always	
Internal Item Master	None	Frequently—usually critical functionality	
Vendor Performance Measurement	Minimal—usually by contract	Almost always—variable measurement criteria	

Source: Gartner, "The MRD E-Procurement Civil War: Blue vs White," Dan Miklovic & Carl Lenz, February 2000.

with around half of the workload of a typical purchasing department dedicated to these low-value, repetitive orders. The average level of productivity for this area is appalling, and it is one of the most labor-intensive areas of modern business.

Part of the problem is that indirect procurement policies are seldom standardized in large or multisite companies, varying greatly between departments and between branch and corporate office. The accompanying approval policies are usually cumbersome, sometimes requiring multiple levels of sign-off, which causes delays and internal inconvenience when employees wait for needed items and middle-management staff members put off signing burdensome paperwork. In exasperation, approval thresholds are raised, and spending anarchy ensues, with only the larger ticket items falling into an even more stringent and extended approval process.

There is a second area of cost. For most companies, this cumbersome, centralized process is augmented by independent, or *maverick,* buying by employees throughout the organization who buy items—paper, scissors, light bulbs—when needed independently, often at nondiscounted and even retail prices. This maverick buying—that tendency for individuals, or often entire departments, to buy "off-contract" without taking advantage of negotiated company discounts—is often rampant, particularly among larger companies, and typically can account for a staggering average of between 30% and 45% of all indirect procurement spending. *To put the effect of this maverick buying phenomenon into perspective, consider that at these rates a typical billion-dollar company would be losing up to $10 million each year just in lost discounts alone.* The smaller the company, the less formal the process, as a rule, and for those non manufacturing companies that do not see purchasing as a core competency, a frightening 84% of indirect materials are purchased simply by employees visiting their local retail outlet.[4] This "rogue buying" can be a significant cost to companies, and even a modest reduction in maverick purchasing can significantly cut procurement costs.

A DAY IN THE LIFE OF A TYPICAL PROCUREMENT SCENARIO: TODAY

In order to appreciate both the need for e-procurement and why it is so revolutionary, it is only necessary to look at a typical organization's approach to procurement.

Select Goods

Today most companies still have shelves filled with well-thumbed (and often out-of-date) paper catalogs provided to them by the vendor. These are available only to those with direct access (i.e., usually central purchasing) and often require multiple calls and semi-confused conversations between users and the purchasing specialist, and then many other calls to the several suppliers in order to resolve issues on price, availability, and delivery times.

The Requisition Process

Except for those companies whose central purchasing department has direct links to a supplier through EDI, the requisition process is still paper-based, usually with multiple copies of requisition forms sent through internal mail to various managers within the approval chain. Approving managers seldom know if the vendor is "on-contract," or how the purchase will be affected by volume discounts.

Waiting for Approval

In many companies, the approval process then follows two paths: technical and financial, with expensive or unusual items moving up a chain of multiple sign-offs, often with long delays and many explanatory phone calls. I recently worked with a financial services company that was examining its procurement process and that had seven layers of sign-offs for approval of items over $500 for both the technical and the financial sides. The average time for approval for high-cost items was three weeks, but could easily run into months.

Creating the Purchase Order

Once final approval has been given, central purchasing collects the paperwork and the information is transferred—by hand—to a purchase order form and then usually faxed to suppliers. This is generally accompanied by further phone calls to confirm receipt. Copies are sent to shipping and receiving and accounting and finance, and then filed with various department managers.

For most companies, this process remains much the same as it was before World War II (except for the fax, of course); with long and unpredictable cycle times. Although there is usually a strong relationship between purchasing officers and suppliers, particularly for indirect goods, there is little ongoing attempt at strategic sourcing. Often, policies vary or overlap between each office, division, and business unit, or between corporate and departmental levels. There is seldom any means for tracking the progress of the order, nor any formal or standardized system in place to measure relative costs, savings, or vendor performance. Long lead times, particularly with MRO items, cause individuals to stock excess materials, raising inventory levels and carrying costs, and increasing the risk of obsolete stock.

Although in most manufacturing and distribution companies procurement is often a core competency, the process of purchasing direct materials for many companies is frustratingly similar to that of indirect goods. But purchasing direct production materials or MRO is, first and foremost, time sensitive and focused on the hourly demands of the assembly line. Yet, because the process is still paper-based and therefore both sequential and prone to errors, even the most efficient purchasing employees tend to experience a lack of integration between departments, numerous misorders, and gaps in materials delivery. The fear of being caught short forces purchasing officers to carry excess inventory, thereby raising carrying costs. Attempts by the CFO to reduce inefficiency through cost-based accounting and departmental-based incentive programs often create conflicting, silo-based priorities, disrupting the horizontal supply chain process flow, forcing managers back into positions where their department budget becomes more important than overall efficiency or cost of production to the firm.

The same issues concerning strategic sourcing and volume discounts apply to the direct materials side, where purchasing staff often complain of a lack of accurate, up-to-date performance data on what can be hundreds and sometimes thousands of suppliers. All of these issues are simply compounded by the complexity and scale of the procurement process for manufacturing. And yet all excess costs stem, ultimately, from the fact that a paper-based, sequential process, no matter how well-devised and run, can simply not provide a company with a single, accurate forecast, a just-in-time (JIT) materials delivery process, rationalized and minimized safety-stock, and a reliable available-to-promise date. *It is this unpredictability— that the wrong goods are being ordered, that the vendor will not deliver the right items, that the goods will not arrive on time—that is the basis for all excess costs.*

NEITHER DIRECT NOR INDIRECT— JUST E-PROCUREMENT

Until now, the focus of nearly all e-procurement energy, software, and press coverage has been on the indirect materials side of procurement, partly because the purchasing process of high volume, low-unit-cost goods that can easily be bought at a retail store with a credit card are much easier to automate than more complexly engineered MRO or direct manufacturing materials and goods. The in-house software platforms and third-party exchanges and buying hubs that are just now beginning to mature began their focus with indirect procurement, but are quickly shifting toward vertical and horizontal exchanges for suppliers of direct goods. With Enterprise Resource Planning (ERP), Advanced Planning and Scheduling (APS), and independent supply chain software vendors moving quickly into alliances that will help extend a buyer's supply chain back into their supplier's systems, by all accounts, e-procurement will be a major leap toward achieving the—until now, primarily theoretical—"pull" type of relationship that manufacturers would like to have with their suppliers, with vendors able to electronically and automatically "see" through the entire supply chain and take responsibility for inventory and JIT delivery of production materials.

Accordingly, as valuable as the automation of the indirect materials process can be, the real savings for manufacturing, distribution, and retail companies will come in applying those same principles to direct material procurement. *Even now, the traditional division between direct and indirect purchasing is beginning to blur, and the logic of the evolution is toward treating it as one process.*

One strong step in this direction comes when software vendors begin to develop *total procurement* information systems that capture, through advanced data warehousing tools that interrogate ERP and other back-end company systems, all information regarding suppliers and products purchased by the company. Decision support tools such as SAS Solution's Supplier Relationship Management System have emerged that allow companies to access and organize all transactional purchasing information—both direct and indirect—and consolidate them in a single data warehouse. Using business information made available through an arrangement with Dunn & Bradstreet, the system provides relationship information about suppliers—what products were purchased from them, how much those products cost, the name of the supplier's parent company, their delivery and financial performance—all of which provides organizations with the ability to accurately complete strategic sourcing exercises based on real-time, legacy system information.

E-PROCUREMENT VISION OF THE FUTURE: TOMORROW

With e-procurement, life is very different. Any employee can be provided on his or her desktop PC with access to a user-friendly point-and-click system on which he or she can browse through online catalogs of the company's approved vendors. Products can be identified by features or by model numbers or names, and the search will prioritize the results according to how well items match the buyer's requirements. The system will provide a side-by-side comparison of the products. Prices can be compared between suppliers, and discounts calculated easily. Information concerning availability, delivery, and payment of supplies is readily available, and payments can be made electronically.

Approvals for standard supplies are automatic, and exceptions are immediately routed through a list of approval deputies, ensuring that if no response is received in a matter of minutes, the approval is routed quickly to another prenamed deputy. There is a complete audit trail of the request, price, approval, and payment information, and transaction information is captured and recorded for vendor performance analysis. There is an instant update for other interested parties—accounts payable and receiving—and most transactions will take only a few minutes. All purchase order and delivery details are available online for both the supplier and the buyer to see.

This level of functionality, particularly for indirect goods, is already available, although the choice for the infrastructure—maintained as in-house software or outsourced through third-party providers or through online auctions—is still very fluid, and these strategic choices are explored in the following chapters.

The equivalent level of functionality and ease-of-use on the direct materials side of procurement is less universally available now, but that functionality promises to explode in the near-term. The same functionality in terms of electronic requisitioning, online pricing, and streamlined approval exist, of course; but although the potential for purchasing through the growing number of online auctions, reverse auctions, and industry exchanges exists, only the most stouthearted and progressive multinationals have plunged fully into electronic procurement of direct manufacturing materials.

But, whether direct procurement takes place through a third-party or through industry-focused supply portals (which are explored in the following chapters), advanced companies are already able to tap the Internet to source parts globally, manage inventory collaboratively, forecast and plan production and manufacturing starts with key suppliers, and provide transparency between ERP systems so that suppliers can "see" and participate in the planning and execution of manufacturing forecasts. All of this can be done in real time, greatly reducing the need to carry excess safety stock or to maintain complex contractual relationships with preferred vendors.

3M Takes on Indirect Procurement Over the Internet

3M, the diversified manufacturing company headquartered in St. Paul, Minnesota, in the past created hundreds of thousands of invoices each year for indirect supplies at a cost of approximately $120 each. The invoices accounted for more than 70% of the company's transaction volume, but only 2% of total purchasing dollars.

Each requisition took from one to three days to process internally, and 30% of the orders required rework. Between 30 and 45% of the indirect purchases were not in compliance with vendor contracts, adding 20% to the annual costs of goods purchased.

Two years ago, 3M implemented a pilot TPN Marketplace solution (from TPN Register), followed by a staged rollout of the technology through the end of 1999. Now more than 2,000 3M buyers purchase contracted goods from a group of online suppliers. "By leveraging TPN Register's Internet marketplace services," says Kathy Van Keulen, project lead for 3M procurement, "we are gaining control over our indirect spending, increasing on-contract purchases, dramatically lowering transaction costs, and virtually eliminating order-processing errors."

With the internal use of TPN Marketplace increasing, Van Keulen says that 3M anticipates reducing the cost of processing purchase orders 70 percent to an average of just $40 and shaving the internal order cycle time to less than one hour. Because the product and contract information is automatically generated on purchase orders, the error rate is expected to shrink to zero.

In its most perfect state, the simultaneous availability of data to all the parties in the extended supply chain means that—with the elimination of uncertainty, people, and paper—transaction time will be reduced to very little more than the actual time it takes to physically transport the materials. If tight integration can be achieved between well-integrated systems, the need for the now disparate third-party software systems found today in many manufacturing companies—to monitor safety stocks or manage material flow—simply disappears. At best, this can dramatically increase service levels, smooth out the supply chain, and reduce costs.

But for many industry watchers, the benefits and effects go well beyond cost savings. E-procurement becomes the catalyst that will allow companies to finally integrate their supply chains from end to end, from sales to supplier, with shared pricing, availability, and performance data that will allow buyers and suppliers to work to optimum and mutually beneficial prices and schedules. In short, for many people, it is the key to collaborative commerce and success in the extended enterprise—the "Holy Grail" of production specialists everywhere. Fortunately, the question is not whether or not this level of functionality can be achieved; it is more a question for individual companies of how to achieve it, and at what price.

ENDNOTES

1. "E-Procurement: Unleashing Corporate Purchasing Power," ©2001 Time Inc., all rights reserved. www.fortune/sections/eprocurement2000, retrieved July 19, 2000.
2. "E-Procurement: The Transformation of Corporate Purchasing," Time, Inc. in association with AMR Research, Inc., May 2, 2000, ©2001 Time Inc., all rights reserved. www.fortune.com/sections/eprocurement2000, retrieved July 19, 2000.
3. Miklovic, D., and Carl Lenz, "The MRO E-Procurement Civil War: Blue vs White," *Gartner Advisory Research Note, Tactical Guidelines,* The Gartner Group, February, 2000, pp. 2–3; "Survey: How Companies Order MRO Supplies," *Modern Distribution Management,* February 25, 2000, p. 6.
4. "Survey: How Companies Order MRO Supplies," *Modern Distribution Management,* February 25, 2000, pp. 1–2.

3 Understanding the Strategic Nature of E-Procurement

Objective

Too often in the past purchasing has been seen as a tactical, back office activity. But, from now on, it should be viewed as a critical part of a company's overall e-business strategy.

- ERP and APS systems have improved internal company processes.

- E-procurement systems improve the external B2B processes. E-procurement is a matter of strategy first and technology second.

- The idea of automating and integrating the procurement process should have a compelling value proposition for many different corporate officers.

- E-procurement will not only reduce purchasing costs but will help to move manufacturing and distribution firms closer to becoming an extended enterprise, where the supply chain becomes a continuous, uninterrupted process extending from buyer through selling partners.

Most of us would admit that the procurement function has seldom in the past been seen as particularly strategic to an organization's success. This is particularly true of indirect goods and services, where, in squeeze times, executives often press for cost-cutting measures, limited usually to fairly ineffectual changes—restricting first class flights or suggestions that the coffee machines be furnished with less expensive brands. Savings have usually been made through discount negotiations or bulk buying; but even these efforts are often offset by lack of choice and excess carrying costs. It is because we have been so limited in our possible actions in the past—discounting or price reductions—that we have come to view efforts to reduce indirect procurement costs as piecemeal and ultimately of little return for the effort.

Purchasing the goods necessary for the everyday running of a company is usually extraordinarily expensive and laborious, representing between 40% and 60% of total company revenue.

EDI (Electronic Data Interchange): a dedicated electronic connection, usually between buyers and their largest selling partners, used for transfer of purchasing information.

Acquiring direct materials for manufacturing, of course, is a different story. Companies have long sought ways to reduce costs associated with the purchase of materials, with the maintenance and upkeep of machinery, and with the transportation and delivery of finished goods. Purchasing of goods and services has always been seen as an integral part of the supply chain, and attempts at using technology in order to eliminate bottlenecks in the past has led to the widespread use of fax machines and, at least with larger buyers, the introduction of EDI (Electronic Data Interchange) technologies.

In a broader sense, though, during the past two decades, particularly, there has been a consistent and effective focus on productivity improvement—ISO ratings, kanban, cellular manufacturing, strategic sourcing, vendor-managed inventory, JIT manufacturing—all with the view that excessive costs (aside from price and unavoidable transaction costs) stem from missed commitments, poor planning, inconsistent quality of merchandise, and general unpredictability in the relationships between buyer and seller. And, although the potential effects of e-procurement are significant, it is important to remember that driving inefficiency out of the supply chain is part of an ongoing technical and structural revolution, and that as unstoppable as it is, it is not all that revolutionary. In fact, it is probably worthwhile to point out that this "evolutionary" shift has been taking place for the past several decades, and is manifested in several important ways.

First, e-procurement systems continue the trend toward automation of the process and the replacement of human labor through information technology (IT). E-procurement systems automate the requisitioning, approval, shipping, receiving process, and payment systems, and provides for automated routing and tracking capabilities, essentially eliminating the need for human intervention other than on an exceptions-only basis.

Second, e-procurement continues to enhance the breakdown of traditional vertical silos and to shift management's focus toward horizontal processes and the empowerment of individual employees. In the past, the purchasing process was seen as a set of separate activities and functions, controlled centrally or departmentally, often focused narrowly on silo-based incentives rather than on total cost. As part of the tortured but inevitable shift from silo to horizontal processes, e-procurement systems facilitate the viewpoint that direct procurement of materials for finished goods is all part of a single, fully-integrated process, extending from forecasting and planning through to the entire supplier network. For indirect and MRO materials, e-procurement systems allow for a far greater level of individual empowerment as preapproved and fully auditable purchasing is handed over to individual employees.

Finally, e-procurement means a giant leap forward in the long-sought-after development of the extended enterprise, where the supply chain becomes a continuous, uninterrupted process extending from buyer through selling partners. As an integrated set of processes and systems that create a seamless, electronically initiated and monitored exchange of information, goods, services, and payment between buying and selling organizations of all types, e-procurement is integral to a process that can, and should, stretch from the planning and forecasting function of the buying company all the way through to the delivery and payment functions of the selling organization, regardless of the product or service, and whether direct or indirect.

Many progressive companies have always seen procurement as part of this chain of events, of course, but despite that, have seldom organized their business horizontally as a single, multifaceted process—mostly because each step had to be completed individually by skilled humans. Unfortunately, despite our talk of horizontal processes and integrated supply chains, the fact is that e-procurement is still in its infancy, and its effectiveness, particularly for direct materials, is dependent upon integration with other systems. It is also, most importantly, dependent upon not only sharing critical inventory information with suppliers (something few companies do well today) but also on actually integrating the supplier-buyer interface. That is why individual, nonintegrated procurement packages that only provide a focused or partial solution, are so problematic. It is also why integration with a company's back-end Enterprise Resource Planning (ERP) and Advanced Planning and Scheduling (APS) systems becomes so critical.

BACK-END SYSTEMS AND THE MODERN ORGANIZATION

Despite the fact that the IT revolution has been with us now for nearly three decades, the more fundamental restructuring that was promised (and feared) in terms of the replacement of people with systems, has been far less dramatic than expected. This is because, until recently, the effect and focus of IT systems tended to be limited to office automation and accounting. It was only with the introduction of the massive and sophisticated ERP systems that organizations began to use IT systems to fundamentally restructure the way they did work. ERP systems became the backbone and nervous system of the modern organization, responsible for capturing, organizing, and presenting the vast amount of financial, process, and performance information. Although often poorly implemented and less agile than hoped, they had the potential, at least, to fundamentally change the way that large numbers of employees worked in an organization. What is more, without a comprehensive system for collecting key corporate information, all other systems were limited in their scale to piecemeal and departmental functions. For the first time, ERP systems allowed an organization to at least begin to understand, in real time, what was occurring in their many processes—marking the beginning of an entire new era of IT.

APS (Advanced Planning and Scheduling): advanced software platforms that provide demand forecasting and planning, resource scheduling, and production plans.

Unfortunately, in their initial phase, ERP systems did not necessarily produce the return on investment (ROI) or process improvement results that might have been hoped for. Because they were fundamentally designed to collect, organize, and report on financial and manufacturing performance information, they could not help organizations with the next key step—using what they learned from that information to improve their company's performance. For manufacturing and distribution companies, responsibility for forecasting and planning fell to the set of equally sophisticated software platforms that were known as APS systems. Their strength was taking the vast amount of historical and real-time data available and "advising" the company on the most sensible use of resources: demand forecasting and planning, resource scheduling, and production plans. Enormously powerful, these APS systems often overlapped and competed with ERP systems, causing significant and ongoing restructuring through mergers, partnerships, and competitive development between the two groups. But ultimately, they filled a key gap in the evolution of automated systems—the second leg of a three-legged stool.

Yet, although the ERP and APS systems could provide companies with all the information they required to function at an entirely new level of productivity, organizations still lacked the ability to use that information to seamlessly extend their supply chain through purchasing of materials and needed resources through their supplier network. At best, these two systems could coordinate key areas such as manufacturing, planning, and sales, but they did little to extend the supply chain from customer to vendor. After all, it undermines the value of ERP and maintenance management software if, after alerting procurement specialists to the need to reorder critical maintenance parts, the paper-based procurement process itself is too unpredictable to ensure timely delivery. *In short, ERP and APS have greatly improved internal company processes, but have done little to improve external business processes. That is where the Internet, B2B e-commerce, and especially e-procurement systems come in.* They are the third leg of the three-legged stool.

Notice in all of this that despite the hyperbole and market enthusiasm, e-commerce (electronic retailing) as a fundamental step forward in the evolution of the extended enterprise does not figure as prominently as the current market noise level might lead us to expect. It is not that Web pages and portals are not important to established bricks and mortar companies, to the myriad of online dotcoms, and to the economy as a whole, but I suspect that ten years from now we will see e-commerce for what it was—an extension of the advertising and sales channel into individual homes. The real and lasting effect of being able to order, sell, and pay over the Web will come from business-to-business and e-procurement transactions.

It is probably important to point out, however, that on the other hand, e-procurement is not just purchasing done electronically. (I use the terms fairly interchangeably, although some would argue that purchasing is essentially the "buying process," whereas procurement is much broader in scope, covering much of the full order fulfillment supply chain.) The changes that e-procurement demands are fundamental in nature and unique to an age where key procurement information—in the form of item masters, purchase orders, product catalogs, inventory lists, and even payments—can be digitized and distributed simultaneously and instantly to multiple parties electronically, regardless of location. This will mean a significant level of restructuring, and rethinking of the way that companies approach purchasing of both direct and indirect goods. These revisions, in turn, will inevitably lead to significant productivity increases for the global economy as a whole.

THE STRATEGIC NATURE OF E-PROCUREMENT

Over the past several years, I have facilitated many executive workshops concerned with the procurement process. In more recent times, when examining e-procurement as part of a company's overall approach to e-business, I am still surprised to find that when selecting potential attendees for these strategy workshops, the initial reaction by managers and executives alike is to nominate only directors and managers who are directly engaged in day-to-day procurement activity to attend.

The reason is, of course, that many people still view the procurement process as a cumbersome, manual support operation (which, for most companies, it still is)—in any case, not an area to concern top management. Many people once had a similar view of the supply chain, although attitudes have recently changed. After all, for manufacturing and distribution companies, their very existence is dependent on getting the right product, where they want it, at the right time, and at the lowest cost to their company. Business strategy is defining the best way to do that, and procurement plays an increasingly pivotal role in that strategy.

In fact, the idea of automating and integrating the procurement process has a compelling value proposition for many different corporate officers. For the Chief Operating Officer, it means that he or she can get lower cost materials, improve manufacturing throughput, and reduce carrying costs for safety goods. The Chief Procurement Officer is able to better focus on central purchasing, moving them away from the administrative, cost center mentality, and toward becoming a specialist purchasing group, responsible for complex or sensitive vendor negotiations, building supplier relationships, and strategic sourcing.

For the Chief Financial Officer, an e-procurement approach can significantly reduce both price of goods and real transaction costs, while greatly improving the company's overall level of productivity by eliminating the manual, paper-based process. The Chief Information Officer can boast that he or she has brought value to users on the desktop and steered his or her company toward the ranks of the progressive. Finally, it reflects best on the Chief Executive Officer, who appreciates that, in many ways, competition in the future, particularly among manufacturing and distribution companies, hinges on how well the respective companies have organized and implemented their entire e-procurement process (that is to say, supply chain).

In the end, of course, e-procurement is a matter of strategy first and technology second. As we have already seen, e-procurement affects virtually every function in the enterprise, from central purchasing to a company's myriad supplier base. Accordingly, companies need to think about how they want e-procurement to affect their relationships with their suppliers. They need to rethink how they want to organize their entire supply chain—from customer to supplier—and having understood the complex nuances of the current e-procurement marketplace, decide what types of services they want to purchase, outsource, or keep in-house. Only then will they want to begin thinking about hardware or software platforms.

But, more importantly, once implemented effectively for direct materials purchasing, the process will extend directly from customer to supplier instantaneously upon an order, and will for the first time truly provide for a "make-to-order" capacity. This is a huge step forward from simple JIT delivery of materials. The discipline of e-procurement, when seen as the supply chain's key component, means that enormous strides have been made in removing "latency and inertia" in the supply chain itself. It is only when suppliers can "see" into the buyer's supply chain systems, reacting real-time to orders, customized requests, or order changes, that the buyer can confidently promise his or her own customers that they can have customized and rapid service. It means companies can greatly increase service without increasing costs to the customer, and this will become even more critical as companies move more and more toward mass customization.

In short, the e-procurement initiative provides an invaluable opportunity for organizations to restructure themselves and their partner relationships in ways that are fundamental and were never before possible.

STRATEGIC FOCUS OF THE E-PROCUREMENT INITIATIVE

Accordingly, the purpose of any e-procurement initiative should be to

- Improve efficiency and reduce labor costs by eliminating the manual, paper-based processes and providing enterprise-wide, self-service procurement
- Enforce on-contract buying; eliminate maverick buying
- Gather accurate and meaningful data on total spending, both by supplier and type of purchase (decision support)
- Using supplier performance, select preferred suppliers for strategic sourcing
- Move as many transactions as possible to front-line employees without undermining business rules
- "Smooth out" the supply chain: integrate process and systems, internally and with suppliers

Ultimately, possibly one of the most important results of the e-procurement debate will be to highlight to key executives the importance and strategic nature or the procurement process itself and its integral relationship with the supply chain and a company's bottom line.

Making the Business Case for E-Procurement

Objective

As with any major investment of time and resources, an e-procurement initiative should be based upon a strong and well-documented business case.

■ The e-procurement business case comes from three areas: *process efficiencies, compliance,* and *leverage.*

■ Process efficiencies come not only from eliminating paperwork and human intervention, but also from shifting indirect purchasing responsibilities, to the employee desktop.

■ The system reduces maverick buying and ensures compliance to the organization's purchasing guidelines.

■ E-procurement makes it possible to capture accurate and timely information on every purchase.

■ New reporting and decision support tools now help procurement specialists to scrutinize their buying patterns.

New reporting and decision support tools now help procurement specialists to scrutinize their buying patterns, providing more dependable information on performance, compliance, and the effectiveness of comparative buying practices and supplier selection. As we have already seen, there are always two types of cost involved in procurement of materials: first, the cost of the goods

Although there are significant savings to be made through better buying decisions and contract compliance, it is even more important to look at the potential savings to be made from reducing procurement processing or transaction costs through digitizing and streamlining the process, reducing the cycle time, and eliminating unnecessary manual intervention.

themselves, and second, the cost inherent in the process of buying the goods. Accordingly, when making the business case for e-procurement, it is important to look beyond just how the system can help you to shop for competitive pricing or receive consistent discounts from suppliers.

PROCESS EFFICIENCIES

When developing an e-procurement business case, it is important then to look at three areas of focused improvement: process efficiencies, compliance, and leverage.[1] Although you have already begun to get some idea of the scale of process efficiencies that can come from automating the procurement process, it is worth noting that there are several ways that an e-procurement system creates cost savings. The first and most obvious are the savings that come from automating the process, eliminating paperwork and human intervention, and reducing transaction costs and cycle time. These savings come not only from eliminating the errors and time associated with paperwork, but also from streamlining and automating the audit trail and approval process.

The second focus area for efficiency savings is more structural than procedural, and comes from shifting the selection and ordering process back to the employees' desktop, eliminating the multiple purchasing middlemen now involved in everyday indirect goods procurement, and giving the individual employee the choice—and responsibility—for purchasing goods. This not only helps to eliminate maverick buying and ensure broad compliance with purchasing rules, but also reduces the errors traditionally associated with requisition responsibility being passed from person to person through the central purchasing and approval chain. Let's look at each of these areas more closely.

Process Automation Savings

Cost surveys have recently revealed what was suspected for some time: that by the time a requisition makes its way through a fax and internal mail paper maze of approvals to the central purchasing department, administrative costs—typically running from $40 to $150—often exceed the cost of the purchase itself. Accordingly, any good e-procurement software system today is designed to greatly reduce the time and effort required to complete purchasing transactions by eliminating our traditional paper chain of requisitions, approvals, receiving, and payment reconciliation. The key features of most of these e-procurement approaches enable users to find an item in an electronic catalog, create a requisition, have the order requisition routed for approval (if necessary), create and transmit the order to vendors, and (in varying degrees) help to automate the payment and invoicing process.

There are two key elements to this approach. First, the entire procurement process—budgeting, requisitioning, ordering, approval, purchase order development, payment, and delivery—should be completed electronically and, as much as possible, simultaneously, so that there is a minimum of manual intervention or delay. Second, the entire process becomes "rebalanced" so that the hundreds of thousands of ordinary and uncontroversial purchases take place with the minimum of supervision or human intervention, and only "exceptions" are flagged through exception reports for the attention of procurement specialists or management.

At the heart of this system is the online catalog, usually assembled and maintained by the supplier (and, at least today, optionally residing either on the buyer's internal systems or on an external third-party portal). These catalogs provide information such as product descriptions with clear specifications and sizes, availability and lead times, delivery policies, schedules, and the negotiated terms, conditions, and discounted prices of items. The requisition and approval process is activated automatically, and the system then converts the requisition into electronic purchase orders that are automatically integrated into the buyer's ERP and back-end systems. Aside from the catalogs, most good e-procurement systems also then include:

- **Requisitioning.** The system should provide customized supplier lists and electronic catalogs, which can be searched using powerful search engines that help employees to quickly locate what they want to purchase by broad category, part description, or supplier. These databases can be customized by group or department, and include security systems based on passwords and authorization. The system should also provide comparative product and pricing information, online standard forms, contracts, hyperlinks to supplier Web sites and RFPs (Request for Proposal), and user-friendly purchasing negotiation tools for nonspecialists.

- **Approval routing.** All good e-procurement systems provide an automated, e-mail-based approval workflow tool that can be customized around approval parameters and can be set to automatically prioritize according to required date. They also ensure timely approval by electronically appearing on the approving manager's screen, and if no response is received, moving on automatically through a series of deputies.

- **Order management.** This includes consolidated and automated ordering, shipping and reordering, and receiving and invoice approval functions. The requisition numbers and purchase order numbers are automatically reconciled, removing the tedious and inaccurate "rationalization" process that takes up so much employee time today. Paper requisitions totally disappear. Good systems also provide for real-time order tracking and requisition status.

- **Summary billing and consolidated reporting.** The system automatically notifies accounts payable, without having to produce a paper-based invoice or to match against the original requisition form. There is an accurate and auditable posting of all purchases and costs, providing the company with information on committed costs at the instant that they are recorded.

- **ERP and CMM (Computerized Maintenance Management) systems integration.** Most e-procurement systems provide a number of direct links to your company's ERP procurement modules and, if procuring blue collar maintenance (MRO) inventory, can provide much higher accuracy and lower inventory handling costs by exchanging information on forecasts, purchases, inventory levels, and delivery status directly to and from your CMM system.

- **Decision support.** These systems also provide you with flexible reporting options that help procurement specialists capture company spending history by item, person, department, and vendor, providing the information necessary to predict future purchasing trends, estimate workloads, and negotiate better contracts with suppliers.

- **Asset management.** Often not thought of as an essential part of an e-procurement solution, the need to provide end-to-end management of resources, once purchased, and to monitor and anticipate the need for replacement has recently driven many software platforms to include asset and cost management modules. Purchasing, of course, is just the first step in the asset management process, and costs related to delayed orders, long approval times, lost orders, or purchasing IT products with incompatible technologies are increasingly significant—particularly as organizations continue to see hardware and software products proliferate throughout the firm.

The system should be as simple and straightforward as possible, using click-and-order technology with frequently purchased goods bookmarked and each item presented with a color identification photo and a detailed product description. It should be events-based so that it can support recurring events, such as training workshops for which there will be a need for manuals, flip charts, overhead markers, and catering. It should seamlessly transcend multiple supplier and catalog boundaries, and support changes to pricing and promotion materials on a real-time basis. And, finally, it should provide strong workflow direction, including automatic approval deputization, a full audit trail, and instant update of in-house financials and other back-office systems.

Compliance

Rogue procurement, off-contract purchasing, or maverick buying, however described, is an activity that is almost universally accepted as a part of modern business life. Partly because these purchases are so often only for small items, and partly because there is no consolidated record of the total effect of such purchases, few companies appreciate the cost associated with noncontract buying.

In fact, though, figures indicate that the impact of maverick buying on organizations can be surprisingly costly. A recent study indicates that nearly one-third of all ORM (indirect) purchasing was conducted off-contract, at an average cost to the company of between 15% and 27%.[2]

One obvious effect of providing a universally accessible and user-friendly purchasing system—particularly valuable for low-value, high-volume items—is that the responsibility for initiating purchasing transactions is shifted away from the purchasing department and into the hands of front-line users, essentially pushing e-procurement to the individual desktop and freeing up central purchasing specialists for more strategic work. Because the e-procurement software provides for purchasing via preapproved catalogs, purchasing agreements are in place so users know what they are authorized to buy. The system itself reduces maverick buying and ensures compliance to the organization's purchasing guidelines, which in turn means both lower transaction costs and more certain receipt of discounts. The system also provides accurate and comprehensive data on buying, and on the flip side, accurate and timely data on supplier costs and performance. This clarity on purchasing activity—possibly most important of all—provides your organization with the ability to understand the trade-offs between service and price.

This "self-service" model requires a good deal of change management, rethinking your rules, and changing behavior; but is ultimately the key to eliminating redundant processes and maverick buying. Although electronic controls are effective, they are much less obvious than the paper-based requisitions or signed approval slips, and at the outset, may be a little below the comfort level of some managers. If your company is like most of the other companies that have adopted these systems, with access to the Internet at the desktop, individuals will quickly begin buying through the approved Web sites and using a variety of electronic marketplaces. But as long as managerial controls are maintained, the ability to purchase via approved suppliers and under pre-negotiated contract terms is assured.

MICROSOFT AND MS MARKET

MS Market is Microsoft's® intranet-based corporate procurement application that provides employees with the tools they need to place orders for products and services, easily and efficiently, from the convenience of their desktops. Linking directly with SAP R/3, Microsoft's current enterprise resource planning solution, MS Market streamlines order processing, facilitates efficient billing, and reduces administrative overhead. By simplifying Microsoft's corporate procurement processing, MS Market has helped reduce per-order processing costs from $60 to $5—saving the company over $7.3 million each year.

Like other companies in today's competitive marketplace, part of Microsoft's success stems from continuing efforts to contain operating costs while providing employees with leading-edge materials and services they need to be productive. Prior to 1996, Microsoft's corporate procurement process relied on dozens of paper forms and multiple custom applications for purchasing goods and services. Processing the wide variety of online and paper order forms was costly, inefficient, and prone to manual data-entry error, in addition to being difficult for both employees and suppliers to manage order delivery and payment.

With thousands of weekly purchase requests of less than $1,000 each, high-volume, low-cost transactions represented 70% of Microsoft's corporate procurement business. Significant resources were dedicated to processing these transactions, including redundant manual data-entry.

In July 1996, an innovative new Web-based application named MS Market was launched to Microsoft employees. MS Market is an online ordering system that works on Microsoft's intranet. It provides employees with easy-to-use, online order forms for office supplies, computer hardware, business cards, catering, vendor contracts, business shipping, and travel services. MS Market validates information such as pricing, ensures that each order is linked to the appropriate accounting code, and automatically routes orders to managers for approval notification via e-mail. According to Lisa Haistings, Senior Product Manager, Corporate Procurement, "We developed MS Market specifically to streamline requisitioning processes and allow us to leverage high-volume transactions to negotiate better pricing with our suppliers." Worldwide, MS Market handles over 400,000 transactions and more than US$5 billion per year in company orders. Microsoft uses the volume of transactions to negotiate discounted pricing with selected suppliers, for additional savings to the company.

Revolutionizing Procurement Processing

Within the first year of operation, MS Market helped the Corporate Procurement Group reallocate 17 of the 19 employees that were previously responsible for processing orders, allowing them to focus on analyzing procurement data and negotiating volume discounts with vendors. In just over four years of operation, MS Market has saved the company millions of operations dollars, improved the ability to negotiate volume discounts from suppliers, and reduced per-order administrative costs from US$60 to just $5.

In addition, MS Market has dramatically changed the way employees manage business requisitions and allocate company resources. Employees now place orders online, typically in less than 3 minutes, without being burdened by administrative paperwork and cumbersome bureaucratic processes. The success of MS Market has led Microsoft to include a technical template for the application with Site Server, Commerce Edition, along with sample sites that can be used to set up custom e-commerce intranet-based solutions. "MS Market has contributed greatly to reducing corporate procurement costs," noted Haistings. "In the past four years, it has saved Microsoft a total of US$18 million dollars."

Source: microsoft.com/business/ HowMicrosoftWorks/casestudies/ msmarket.asp. Portions reprinted with permission from Microsoft Corporation.

The very fact that indirect, and particularly ORM goods, are so easy to select and buy, of course, makes this area the first to be targeted for streamlining and automation. As you will see in Chapter 5, there is a logical progression in terms of software and support offerings that for the past two years has focused on straightforward indirect purchasing, but is quickly shifting toward the more complex purchasing decisions of MRO and direct materials.

Leverage

One of the most important and beneficial effects of an e-procurement framework is that, for the first time, business information systems are so well integrated that they can provide an organization with the key total cost data that allow them to make considered decisions on purchases, discount requirements, and supplier partnerships. In many ways, it is only now that the Internet and advanced software systems make it possible to capture accurate and timely information on every purchase, that companies can analyze complex buying patterns and make truly informed decisions on strategic sourcing options.

Accordingly, one of the most important advantages that come from an e-procurement infrastructure is that robust new reporting and decision support tools now help procurement specialists to scrutinize their buying patterns, providing more dependable information on performance, compliance, and the effectiveness of comparative buying practices or supplier selection. A key area, for example, in the global supply chain, is often-overlooked extra costs or cost savings associated with customs duties or export taxes. Purchasing an item from China less expensively may result in a customs tax that negates the savings, while paying more for the same item from a second country, even at a higher price, might mean an overall savings.

Accordingly, reporting capabilities should

- Provide a better understanding of users' behavior.
- Strengthen relationships with vendors.
- Accurately record vendor performance.
- Reduce off-contract or maverick buying.
- Provide exact figures on process cost.
- Calculate any legal or tax consequences of the purchase.

Not only does this allow for better strategic and tactical buying, but all of this frees up staff to work on other things, including analyzing best performance, working with suppliers to improve cost-effective relationships, and renegotiating performance rewards.

STRATEGIC SOURCING

Over the past decade, particularly, one of the ways that companies were encouraged to overcome a myopic focus on price and to concentrate on true costs was strategic sourcing, which in many ways amounted to little more, at times, than vendor rationalization. These efforts at strategic sourcing are predictable—survey purchasing categories, trawl through the company's purchasing history in order to create a list of the vendors currently being used, reduce the number of suppliers, and then renegotiate prices with the remaining preferred vendors—if not always sustainable, and have been notoriously ineffectual over the long run. Specialist needs, new discount offers, friendly sales representatives, and urgent spot buys soon meant that vendor categories blurred and the supplier ranks grew again. Employees began to demand second-choice auto rental options and senior executives exempted themselves from restrictions on flying first class. The real problem was that no one ever understood or believed in the numbers. It is only when costs, performance measurements, and comparisons can be made accurately and in real time, with an unambiguous audit trail, that the benefits of strategic sourcing can be sustained. It is the combination of certainty of cost and performance data and the availability of decision support tools that allow companies to truly understand which sourcing options are the most effective.

On the other hand, for those firms that can resolve this contradiction internally, new e-procurement strategic sourcing and decision support tools can now free up procurement specialists' time and provide them with valuable information, both on internal spending and on supplier performance. The SAS Institute, for example, provides strategic sourcing and data-mining tools that allow users to understand exactly what, how, and from whom the company is buying, and at what price. This information can then be compared with supplier financial or delivery performance. This gives procurement specialists an opportunity to understand much more clearly the total procurement costs—to look at spending patterns and to analyze where the company is being hit with major price discrepancies or transaction costs. They can then renegotiate contracts or change the purchasing practices, as necessary.

ATLAS SERVICES AND TRADEC

Irvine, California-based Atlas Services is a subsidiary of VEBA Electronics. The company provides semiconductor programming, consignment/stores, automatic replenishment, manufacturing management, prototype support, and vendor-managed inventory services throughout North America, Europe, and Asia.

In March 1999, the company conducted a detailed process study of its quotations group to quantify the benefits of the TRADEC.com e-procurement system it had implemented from San Jose, California-based TRADEC.com.

Atlas' quotations group services all of its North American business. Requests for quotation (RFQs) are routed to a central processing location from local offices across the country. The group typically generates 18 to 20 proposals per month, with the average bill of materials (BOM) consisting of 300 line items. Atlas' supply chain consists of more than 300 suppliers, with 25 of these considered "preferred." Preferred suppliers quote the majority of the RFQs, with the remaining 275 suppliers receiving only occasional RFQs.

To quantify the benefit of the e-procurement system, a business process approach was used. First, the original business process was mapped, and critical data points were identified. Data points included the time spent by individuals on each process step.

Data was gathered for four weeks, using both the original process and e-procurement system. The original (manually based) quote process included 17 process steps, 51 faxes, and 3 data re-entries. Quote turnaround time is defined as the total time from when a system original equipment manufacturer (OEM) sends an RFQ to the time that quotation is returned to the OEM.

At the end of the four-week period, the data was analyzed using two methods: full-cost allocation and activity-based costing. Full-cost allocation assumes that 100 percent of each individual's time was spent processing RFQs; activity-based costing measures the cost of each step in the process based on the time actually spent performing the step. The result is a high-contrast snapshot of the power of e-procurement.

With standard procurement: The average quote turnaround time under the original process was found to be nine business days—with a maximum of 15 business days. Using the standard procurement method, the quotations group spent 10 percent of the nine-day process (i.e., approximately one day) preparing and sending the RFQ to suppliers. They spent another 8 percent analyzing the returned quotations and preparing a proposal for the system OEM. The interim time—82 percent—was spent waiting for supplier responses. More than seven of the nine days were outside the quotation group's control. The original quotation process used a staff of six quote administrators. With full allocation, the average cost of preparing a proposal was $868. With the average BOM being 300 line items, the average cost of quoting a line item was $2.89.

With e-procurement: After implementation of the TRADEC system, the number of process steps was reduced from 17 to 13. Faxes and data re-entry were eliminated. The total time spent handling the RFQ by the quotations group was reduced from 17.7 hours to 9.2 hours, an improvement of 48 percent. The quote turnaround time was reduced from 9 to 6.5 days, an improvement of 27 percent. Of the time saved, 40 percent came from internal processes while 60 percent came from faster supplier response. On an activity basis, the total cost of processing an RFQ was reduced from $204 to $67, a 67 percent improvement.

Several months after completion of the study, the results were further validated when the quotations group was able to grow their business while simultaneously reducing their staff by 50 percent. Today a staff of three handles a greater workload than the original staff of six. (The other quote analysts have been redeployed to other areas within the company).

With full cost allocation, the average cost of preparing a proposal is now $434, or $1.44 per line item—a 50 percent reduction over standard procurement.

Other benefits cited by Atlas include increased accuracy and higher job satisfaction among quote analysts. "The TRADEC system eliminates many of the mundane tasks conducted by quote analysts," says Jim Smith, president of Atlas Services, North America. "Now they can concentrate on building relationships, providing customer service, and thinking strategically—all of which are more satisfying."

Source: Weil, Marty, "Buying Into e-Procurement," *MSI: a B2B magazine about IT for Manufacturing Management*, May 2000, v.10, i5, p. 47.

Many contend, though, that with the development of exchanges and auctions, the very notion of the advantages of strategic sourcing is challenged. It is certainly true that the more suppliers involved in a bid, the more likely you are to be able to negotiate a better overall deal, and particularly for low-cost, high-volume purchases of indirect materials, strategic sourcing and vendor rationalization may be working against competitive forces. After all, if competition is supposed to result in commodity pricing, the more vendors the better. This is particularly true since there will be no longer a need for a "relationship" or negotiated discounts.

THE CHANGING ROLE OF PROCUREMENT SPECIALISTS

One key area of change is that of the traditional purchasing role and the changes to traditional centralized versus decentralized purchasing strategies. They may essentially become one, at least for MRO, except for a small number of overseeing procurement specialists. This elimination of labor and reduction in cycle time can and will be enormous in terms of savings.

One thing that is certain is that the role of the purchasing professional will change dramatically over the next few years (see Figure 4.1). There is a good deal of speculation as to what this role might become. Certainly, any position that currently deals with paper-based transactions will be gone, and depending on how extensively a company pursues a strategy of buying via the impersonal e-markets

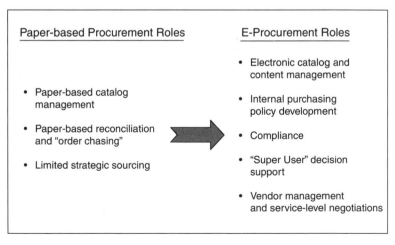

Figure 4.1 The changing role of procurement specialists.

and third-party trading hubs, the role of relationship manager will change dramatically. If a policy of close vendor ties for mission-critical direct materials continues, and strategic sourcing continues to be important, there will always be a role for specialists who understands the manufacturing process and the comparative merits of various material and substitutes.

There will also be a need for purchasing officers with good client management skills to focus not only externally on the buyer-seller relationship (contract management and strategic sourcing), but also internally, within their own firms, to ensure communication and purchasing policy effectiveness throughout the organization. Similarly, there is likely to be a need for specialists who can help develop and continuously update the rules that govern the relationships between suppliers and their companies. Someone—often a person these days known as a *super user*— will need to master the sophisticated decision-support tools that are becoming available in order to advise and help set the buying criteria themselves. To these we can also safely add roles for employees working on catalog management and, whatever the potential of a self-governing "self-service" procurement system, someone working on managing, or at least overseeing, compliance.

Strategic team-based purchasing is the one approach that has developed in the past several years that promises to be enhanced by this shift toward online procurement, because the rationalization of the purchasing process that takes place during an e-procurement initiative tends to help purchasing specialists to view the process by which they acquire direct materials, particularly, as much more horizontal and seamless. The certainty of monitoring compliance that comes from the e-procurement systems also means that procurement specialists in different departments now view purchasing as a corporate rather than a unit function.

ENDNOTES

1. These three categories were first used, to my knowledge, by Price-WaterhouseCoopers in describing e-procurement savings, and still seem very appropriate.
2. Billinge, Colin, 'Everyone Needs a Leader,' in "Understanding E-Procurement," *The Financial Times*, Winter 2000, p. 14.

The E-Procurement Software Landscape

Objective

In order to better understand the current trends in Internet-based e-procurement, it is important to review several of the key events that have occurred in the evolution of e-procurement so far:

- E-procurement came about in the late 1990s as an improvement of EDI technologies and as a way to conduct purchasing transactions over the Internet.

- Originally based on electronic catalogs, the complexities of catalog maintenance quickly gave rise to third-party hosting.

- With the expansion of software capabilities, the original one-to-many model gave way to a second, many-to-many model of procurement.

- The many-to-many model then provided the impetus for entry into the e-procurement arena of many new and powerful parties.

For anyone following the whirlwind developments of the e-procurement world—and that should be nearly everyone in business these days—the e-procurement marketplace must seem incredibly volatile and uncertain. There are sell-side and buy-side application suites, e-procurement networks, vertical and horizontal exchanges, and third-party e hubs and portals. How can anyone make sense out of the seemingly endless mix of these e-business offerings?

To appreciate the complexity and volatility of this marketplace—and also the potential levels of profit up for grabs—it is only necessary to look at the number and types of organizations that are rushing to take part.

To try to add some clarity around the situation, it can help to simply look back over the e-procurement landscape as it developed over the past few years in order to better understand these market machinations.

THE STORY SO FAR

EDI (Electronic Data Interchange): a dedicated electronic connection, usually between buyers and their largest selling partners, used for transfer of purchasing information.

It is only necessary to go back a few years to enter into pre-e-procurement history. Prior to 1997, electronic exchange of information concerning purchasing was pretty much limited to either faxed purchase orders, or for a select group of large and progressive companies, to Electronic Data Interchange (EDI). In fact, for most people in business, EDI is still synonymous with electronic procurement. It is true that large companies have been using EDI with their major trading partners for almost 25 years now, but these EDI systems were based on leased lines, were expensive to establish and to use, and were

d by a lack of agreed-upon standards—most of which were
d for, and therefore proprietary to, certain industries. What is
has always been too complicated and too expensive for
enterprises to set up a dedicated EDI connection (the cost
between $25,000 and $40,000), and as the global economy
to its current phase, it became apparent that EDI would be
complex and cumbersome to exploit the extended enterprise
and global trading communities that were emerging.

E-procurement really began in the late 1990s when several start-up software companies, led particularly by Ariba and Commerce One, began to develop a suite of applications that allowed vendors to create electronic catalogs. It began inauspiciously enough. Most of those original software providers, still unaware of the impending explosive growth of the Internet, created products that, although capable of transmitting over the Internet, would still reside within the firewalls of the buyer company, and were for the most part focused on ORM and MRO types of vendor products. Because vendors seldom had either the skills or IT capacity internally to create or maintain those electronic catalogs, these software suites were primarily designed from a "buy-side" point of view, and responsibility for content management, daily maintenance, and troubleshooting, all fell to the buyer's staff.

However, loading and managing large, and often badly organized, supplier parts information in electronic catalogs turned out to be much more time consuming and difficult than the buyers had originally bargained for. It suddenly became the responsibility of the buyer company's staff to deal with the complexities of aggregating the content of multiple vendors' catalogs, revising and cross-matching prices against discounted service agreements, and constantly updating and editing product changes.

Moreover, not only were there no agreed-upon standards for content management and presentation, but there were no agreed-upon standards for communicating over the fast-growing Internet. Initial attempts to shift EDI to the Internet had proved equally difficult, and even by 1998, a study by the Aberdeen Group concluded that not a single organization they surveyed had been able to connect more than a handful—10 to 15 suppliers—electronically to their systems.[1]

It soon became apparent that this original buyer-managed model would never be successful, because the burden on the buyer's staff was simply too great. Realizing this, several of the e-procurement software companies stepped forward and offered to take on the responsibilities for maintaining the catalogs on behalf of the buyers—essentially providing an outsourcing service on behalf of many vendors and large buyers. They would customize and maintain the catalogs, coordinate communication methods, and then either update the buyer's server on a regular basis via downloads through the Internet, or alternatively, would simply host the catalogs on their own servers, which they would then share with buyers through a Web site portal. They therefore became the intermediaries between the buyer hub and the vendor spokes.

It didn't take the industry long to realize that they were on to a good thing here, and several companies soon began to offer complete outsourcing services, which included developing and maintaining registries of preferred suppliers, and even going so far as to provide contractual and legal services, performance management tools, and logistics support.

This shift toward third-party hosting, of course, was the spark that ignited the explosive and volatile expansion of the entire e-procurement industry. In a short period of time—less than two years—a dramatic change occurred. Instead of focusing on internally held software that buyers had to maintain—or pay to have maintained—buyers and vendors could be provided the same service over the Internet through portals on a subscription basis. Moreover, with the responsibility for catalog management no longer sponsored and controlled by a single buyer, it was a logical next step to make those catalogs available on a similar outsourced basis to many buyers who had similar supplier needs.

This brought about two changes that would alter the e-procurement industry forever. The first was that the *one-to-many* model, which had been the basis for all e-procurement systems designs, suddenly shifted into a *many-to-many* mode. The idea of a hub-spoke relationship in which a single organization would arrange to electronically procure goods from a handful of preferred suppliers (essentially the EDI model moved to the Internet) was suddenly rendered obsolete. Although it still proved attractive to a number of large companies with specific supplier needs, for the most part, the proprietary company extranet—at least as far as e-procurement was concerned—had suddenly and unexpectedly become an anachronism.

ASP (Application Service Provider): a third-party host that provides Web-based services.

The second change—which went hand-in-hand with the realization that a hosted, many-to-many model was infinitely more logical and profitable than a one-to-many model—was the remarkable explosion in electronic marketplaces, online auctions, industry portals, and trading hubs that came about over the span of a few months. These specialist e-markets and third-party trading hubs blossomed in virtually every industry vertical—automotive, energy, petrochemical, steel—as well as in many horizontal markets, such as office supplies and travel services. There are today third-party providers that host virtual shopping malls, online trading exchanges with various types of online auctions, and innumerable types of hosted services—Application Service Providers (ASPs)—that furnish full Web-based e-procurement and e-fulfillment services. Each of these providers serves as a central electronic site that brings suppliers, distributors, and buyers together over the Internet, often boasting a bewildering array of services, including dynamic pricing, Customer Relationship Management (CRM), arbitration and negotiations, and full e-fulfillment.

Added to the complexity of this ever-changing marketplace are the many new and powerful parties that have plunged into the morass. These include the original e-procurement software houses, various newcomers, an assortment of Internet service providers, the major ERP vendors, the large and influential supply chain management software suites, catalog maintenance providers, and a broad array of technical support organizations that provide translation, interface, and interoperability services. There are also—for many of the vertical exchanges—large and financially powerful industry representatives who are busy aligning with various support partners in multibillion dollar collaborative exchanges. Apart from millions in venture capital funding, these collaborative efforts are often given additional financial backing by large international banking concerns.

To appreciate the complexity and volatility of this marketplace—and also the potential levels of profit up for grabs—it is only necessary to look at the number and types of organizations that are rushing to take part.

E-PROCUREMENT SOFTWARE SPECIALISTS

At the heart of the e-procurement revolution are several companies that over the past few years have been building increasingly powerful and flexible software platforms specifically dedicated to online procurement. These include increasingly familiar names, such as Ariba, Commerce One, ProcureNet, Intelisys Electronic Commerce (now Metiom), Sun Microsystem/Netscape, and Broadvision, to name a few, many of which originally developed online procurement software suites that were intended to help usually large and financially powerful companies to develop dedicated, one-to-many enterprise systems. Companies such as Concur Technologies, Clarus, Trilogy, and Remedy all provide "light" systems for the mid-size and smaller company market.

These software suites have all the basic procurement functionality that you might expect. They allow for online catalogs, which today can be managed either by the vendors, by the buying enterprise, or more often these days by ASPs or other third-party groups. They allow employees, either from central purchasing or from the desktop, to electronically search for items; compare prices, functions, and availability; choose different payment methods; requisition the materials; and track materials delivery.

As we have seen, these suites originally focused on the much more straightforward purchase of indirect goods, but lately have moved into providing more advanced functionality for the complex purchasing of direct

CRM (Customer Relationship Management): a software platform that provides customer history, order tracking, and sales information online to customer service agents.

materials. As this drive toward direct materials continues, these companies are beginning to form alliances with providers of supply chain support applications, including those that can round out their e-procurement solutions with CRM, strategic sourcing, or advanced planning and scheduling (APS) functionality. Ariba, for example, purchased Supplier Market.com, an online workplace for manufacturing materials, which it intended to use as part of its direct sourcing infrastructure. Similarly, Commerce One has teamed up with Aspect Development, Extricity, Andersen Consulting, and other partners to create a direct-materials portal.

The major e-procurement players have also all begun to develop a two-pronged approach to implementation that reflects the shift from the one-to-many to the many-to-many model. Not only do they provide a software platform that can be maintained by the buying enterprise (one-to-many), but they now also provide a separate platform that exists as an independent "network" (many-to-many model). For example, Ariba provides an enterprise suite—ORMS (Operating Resource Management Systems)—and also a subscription-based, e-community portal network through its Ariba Network Platform. Commerce One's enterprise solution is BuySite, and its networked e-community platform is MarketSite. Metiom (formerly Intelisys) has the ConnectTrade product suite for both its enterprise and network offerings.

As we have already seen, these networked platforms provide an independent, portal-based trading community that often supports thousands of suppliers with most of the same level of functionality as the enterprise procurement platforms, including requisitioning, tracking, and payment services. These networked solutions, both sponsored by the software creators and sold to independent groups (third-party ASPs and market creators) interested in using these network portals to develop their own industry exchanges, have been instrumental in the explosive growth of vertical trading communities. As these network solutions have become more popular, their functionality has been expanded to include important business services, such as content management tools, integrated payment systems, easy vendor registration, advanced search and comparison tools, strategic sourcing and decision support systems, and other key business support services. Commerce One's MarketSite, for example, also includes payment services from American Express, tax assistance and tools, and logistics and freight delivery services prearranged with UPS and TanData Corp.

The great advantage of these networked offerings is that they provide even small and medium-sized third-party sponsors with essentially a "ready-made" trading community platform. This type of opportunity has been enhanced even more lately, as specialist vendors use their memberships in horizontal network exchanges—such as Ariba's Internet Business Exchange, designed to provide a horizontal platform with full exchange and e-procurement functionality—in order to develop their own industry-specific vertical exchanges within those horizontal networks. Known as *on-ramps,* these exchanges allow members of any size to build up their market-specific content and supplier catalogs—essentially developing their own trading community while never having to build or take responsibility for ownership of the software themselves.

ERP SUPPLIERS AND E-PROCUREMENT

Lumbering along with (and slightly behind) these procurement specialist companies are the many ERP suppliers. These giants—SAP, Oracle, PeopleSoft, Baan, J.D. Edwards, and others—have a long history of providing procurement functionality, because purchasing was an integral part of their supply chain modules that have been developed over the years to integrate with Material Requirements Planning (MRP) and Computerized Maintenance Management (CMM) systems. Not only do ERP suites provide financials (general ledger, accounts payable, accounts receivable, etc.), but they also specialize in automating functions throughout the supply chain (warehouse management, procurement, manufacturing, order processing, etc.), and so provide both the transaction backbone and data source for decision support systems.

Their extensive supply chain and procurement expertise, although never based on Internet technologies in the past, nonetheless gives them reason to claim that their software platforms are the rightful place for procurement functionality, particularly—because their systems provide the backbone for both supply chain and financials—if it involves complex procurement and replenishment of direct materials for manufacturing companies. They also claim a rightful inheritance to e-procurement participation because not only have ERP software suites traditionally contained a good deal of procurement functionality, but in order to be effective, any e-procurement system will still need to tie directly into the ERP systems of both buyers and sellers in order to track order receipts and payments.

Accordingly, there has recently been a scramble for strategic alliances between all the major ERP and e-procurement software vendors. For example, ProcureWorks integrates with Oracle, PeopleSoft, and SAP; and Ariba has a three-way partnership with i2 (tying into its TradeMatrix supply chain software) and IBM, which provides a transaction engine with its WebSphere Commerce offering. Ariba also has partnerships or alliances with PeopleSoft, Oracle, and J.D. Edwards. Commerce One supports SAP's ERP suite under its Global Trading Web portal.

Worth noting also is that both Oracle and PeopleSoft have already begun to pursue a bold dual strategy—integration with major e-procurement suites and a parallel strategy of building their own e-procurement capability. PeopleSoft has a standalone e-procurement product that is tightly integrated with its ERP and financial modules, and Oracle boasts of interoperability with other e-procurement packages, but also has a strategy of providing a variety of Internet-enabled procurement products, such as Oracle Exchange.com, a marketplace that supports procurement for indirect materials.

Supply chain management specialists have also joined the race to produce e-procurement platforms. i2, for example, leverages its knowledge and software designed for direct procurement (TradeMatrix Procurement Services), and apart from its alliance with IBM and Ariba, also has merged with Aspect Development for even greater MRO and direct materials purchasing capability. Metiom and Manugistics, the manufacturing and supply chain decision support software group, announced an alliance designed to help sellers and buyers integrate their e-procurement and supply chain capabilities.

During the past few years, the development of powerful forecasting and planning tools has brought important productivity advances to the manufacturing sector. Over the past decade, demand forecasting has moved from a rudimentary dependency on historical production data used to predict broad, macro trends to a much more sophisticated approach to forecasting and planning production needs using causal data (promotions, seasonal changes, etc.). Today's powerful APS systems—Manugistics, SynQuest, Numetrix, and many others—can now provide a firm with sophisticated, real-time, computer-driven predictions for production and purchasing demand driven by actual sales or distribution needs. As sales force automation or online order fulfillment systems capture orders, these are now transmitted directly via the Web, essentially providing a "pull" for the purchasing and manufacturing groups. These systems therefore complete what is essentially the full automation of the supply chain, greatly reducing the need to maintain costly safety stock because of uncertainty about demand. Of course, to create this type of fully collaborative supply chain, a firm needs to tightly integrate a suite of products that extends from sales force automation through to forecasting tools, the ERP backbone, the online e-procurement system, and ultimately, into the suppliers' systems.

For this reason, another group of software vendors—those involved in planning and forecasting—have entered the direct e-procurement scene, with companies such as i2, Manugistics, and any number of point of sale (POS) vendors now joining alliances with other platforms to complete the Internet-based supply chain (see Figure 5.1).

Moreover, because in the future customers will both initiate and drive their own purchases through the entire supply chain, and because instant or customized sales require customer service agents to be able to provide real-time availability and delivery information to customers, CRM systems are now being seen as critical to the full integration of the e-procurement process. In fact, in great measure because of the interrelated nature of CRM with the growth of B2B e-commerce market, the CRM marketplace is predicted to have a sweeping renaissance, growing from $2.3 billion in 1998 to $16.8 billion in 2003.[2] For that reason, there have been any number of moves by both e-procurement and ERP vendors to align with CRM platforms.

TRANSLATION AND CONNECTIVITY

Recognizing that many companies will want to pick and choose among several e-procurement systems, ERP suites, supply chain systems, and portal platforms, companies such as Extricity and Web-Methods have developed XML-based solutions that integrate these various platforms and applications. Both Ariba and SAP use Web-Methods and other third-party packages to link suppliers and partners, and to provide for additional third-party software links. Others, such as Neon and Lotus, provide adapters or converters specifically designed to integrate various leading procurement and Internet applications. PeopleSoft has its Open Integration Framework (OIF), which uses XML to integrate its ERP modules with other products; Oracle uses the Open Applications Groups' XML methodology to add third-party software links to its ERP solutions; and IBM uses its own B2B Integrator software to tie into third-party software.

Many industry observers continue to point to Microsoft as an up-and-coming key member of the e-procurement community of vendors, not only because of its MS Market online procurement suite, but also because, for many customers, compatibility with the Microsoft business software platforms is essential in order to provide a procurement functionality directly to the employee desktop. One

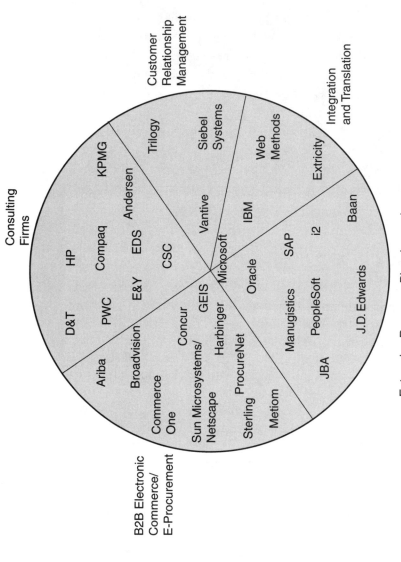

Figure 5.1 Vendors competing in the business-to-business landscape.

of the biggest selling points touted by Clarus, for example, is it focus on Microsoft technologies. Microsoft's BizTalk is an XML based product that allows interconnectivity between Microso; products and ERP systems, portals, and a variety of third-part applications. Microsoft is working closely, however, to also integrat_ Ariba's XML schemas (cXML) into the BizTalk XML framework, and Ariba's ORMs procurement application runs on the Microsoft platforms.

PAYMENT SYSTEMS

Finally, there has also been a rush to integrate into the e-procurement solution a method for secure and easy-to-use electronic payments. This has meant a similar scramble among e-procurement software vendors and ERP companies to form collaborations with major financial services groups, which has revitalized the lagging market demand for the corporate purchasing card.

It is not difficult to see the value of these online payment systems. In fact, it is absolutely critical to the overall effectiveness of any e-procurement initiative, simply because there can be no purchase without payment. Imagine, for example, the difficulties of continuing to pay your vendors on a monthly basis by paper checks. Not only is the paper-based system cumbersome and expensive (a typical large company may cut as many as 1,000 checks each month for indirect materials alone), but without corporate purchasing cards, the e-procurement process becomes—at least for a short time—manual and disjointed again. A simple payment card, assigned to an individual employee with a personal PIN, is both convenient and secure.

A recent survey conducted by the National Association of Purchasing Management on behalf of Visa USA found that nearly one-third of companies that have adopted e-procurement systems already use purchasing cards, and another 57% intend to incorporate purchasing card technology in the future.[3]

Accordingly, developments have continued apace, and most e-procurement systems now boast one or several alliances with large credit card and financial transaction companies for both online payment reconciliation and distribution of corporate purchasing cards to employees. For example, SAPMarkets will use the American Express Corporate Purchasing Card, and Mastercard will provide

PURDUE MOVES TOWARD PURCHASING CARDS

To streamline its automated e-procurement system, Purdue [University] will distribute MasterCard-branded purchasing cards that limit the amount individuals can spend. About 1,000 users in four major areas of the university—the chemistry school, aviation technology school, physical facilities maintenance plant, and the North Central campus in Westville, Indiana—will receive the cards at the program's launch.

After a successful completion of a three-month pilot, Purdue plans to roll out the cards to 2,000 more users a month. By the time the Purdue system is fully implemented, 15,000 faculty and staff members will be able to use a Web browser for requisition and approval of various commodity items.

"The system implementation is the easy part; the hard part is the culture change, the process change, and the enhancement of the security foundation," Purdue's Mike Courtney [manager of the procurement redesign project] says. "This is the first Web-based administrative system to be implemented by Purdue."

The goal: eliminate 80% of paper processes within the first two years.

Source: Greenemeier, Larry, "Buying Power," *Informationweek Online*, April 3, 2000, pp. 3-4. Used with permission.

online payment services to e-procurement solutions from Microsoft, Clarus, and Commerce One. Bank of America has formed an alliance with NIC Commerce to provide electronic payment and purchasing services to state and local governments in the U.S. These payment card programs will provide a network of global merchant credit approval, purchasing control features by card, and detailed line-item reports on use—all of which will help firms to monitor and better understand their purchasing activity.

FINDING YOUR WAY THROUGH THE MINEFIELD

This sudden explosion of activity has left a multitude of business opportunities and is proving to be a boon to the economy globally. But it also leaves many dazed and wondering what to do next. Many questions arise:

- Are all one-to-many structures truly obsolete, or does it still make sense for some organizations to have a dedicated—even if outsourced—procurement hub?

■ Do these e-markets work only for indirect and MRO materials, or are they a feasible system for procuring mission-critical direct goods?

■ What should your policy in the future be on strategic sourcing and vendor management, when third-party exchanges eliminate any personal relationship in the future between supplier and buyer?

■ With more than a thousand electronic exchanges now active, will there soon be a period of consolidation fueled by failures, buy-outs, and mergers?

■ If so, is it safe to invest the future of your company in an e-procurement strategy now, or can you afford to wait?

Although many of these questions simply can't be answered with any degree of certainty at this time, one of the best ways to begin to understand your options is to better understand the architecture of e-procurement itself.

ENDNOTES

1. "E-Procurement: Unleashing Corporate Purchasing Power," Time, Inc., ©2001 Time Inc., all rights reserved. www.fortune.com/sections/eprocurement2000, retrieved July 19, 2000.
2. Baljko, Jennifer, "Software Firms Seek to Move Beyond ERP," www.ebnews.com, October 14, 1999.
3. "E-Procurement: The Transformation of Corporate Purchasing," Time, Inc. in association with AMR Research, Inc., May 2, 2000, ©2001 Time Inc., all rights reserved. www.fortune.com/sections/eprocurement2000, retrieved July 19, 2000.

The Architecture of Web-Based Procurement

Objective

Web-based procurement has developed rapidly into several major models, each of which has its relative strengths and weaknesses:

- Corporate e-procurement systems usually have either a buy- or a sell-side focus and provide central procurement and desktop requisitioning ability.

- Electronic catalogs can be managed by suppliers, buyers, or third parties.

- The development of the independent, Internet-based portal has meant the movement away from the one-to-many model of e-procurement.

- Electronic trading communities can focus on vertical and/or horizontal industry markets.

- The need for broader supply chain and procurement services has meant the rapid rise of many ASPs and other third-party support organizations.

Although a few industry watchers were quick to assume that there would be a continuous

Which model is best for your organization? Is it one, or is it a mixture of several?

and inevitable move away from the one-to-many model of e-procurement, the complexity of purchasing materials globally, the different approaches that ORM, MRO, and direct materials purchasing demand, and concerns over security and partnership reliability have all combined to sustain a good deal of interest in the company-sponsored model. Alternatively, particularly for the more straightforward purchasing of ORM materials, impersonal many-to-many model auctions and exchanges provide small and medium-sized companies with an opportunity to forgo complex and costly negotiations with individual vendors, and to use an online exchange, for a subscription fee, to buy goods at bid-down prices.

SELL-SIDE ONE-TO-MANY: THE STOREFRONT MODEL OR SHOPPING MALL

In order to begin to develop a company strategy for this fast-evolving marketplace, it is important to first understand the nuances of the leading models. They take several forms.

First, they have either a *buy-side* focus (designed predominantly to serve the needs of the buying organization) or a *sell-side* focus (sponsored by and most beneficial to suppliers). They are then divided according to whether they have a one-to-many focus or a many-to-many focus. For each of these combinations, there are then several variations in approach. To begin, let's start with the most basic one-to-many model.

In the sell-side one-to-many model (shown in Figure 6.1), sellers create their own Internet sites that allow any number of buyers to browse and purchase their products

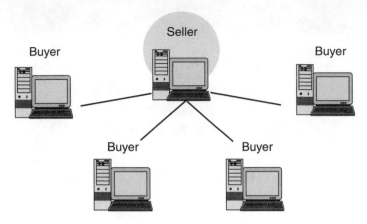

Figure 6.1 Sell–side one–to–many model.

online, with real-time, contract-specific buying. The responsibility for creating and maintaining the catalogs lies with the sellers, and they use an open Web site, or portal, on the Internet to promote what is essentially an online store for their products. Increasingly, they also make their catalogs available to intermediaries (e-markets) either through Internet links or through actual contracts for listing as "preferred suppliers". These e-markets, which we will discuss in a moment, then provide specialized online focus to particular horizontal and vertical industry markets. In many ways, this model is more e-commerce than e-procurement (a method for selling rather than purchasing), except these *storefront* or *shopping mall* portals now provide significant opportunity for buyers to purchase goods online from all over the world.

The obvious advantage for sellers is that they can create and maintain their own catalogs. The disadvantage to the system is that, because the storefront is a common portal, it has in the past been very difficult to integrate well with the buyers' back-end financial systems. This makes life very difficult for the buyers, because nothing is automated from their point of view—they still have to locate the supplier's Web site, log on, and enter orders manually through the catalog Web forms, which, simply because of volume, do not normally retain the buyer's template or company purchasing information. Each buyer must therefore rekey all the relevant profile information—company name, address, telephone numbers, account codes—each time. Obviously, for a company with hundreds of suppliers, this means visiting hundreds of Web sites and continuously rekeying information. To make matters more difficult, the buyer then has to simultaneously update his or her own internal ERP system. Although this approach has obvious advantages over the pure paper-based catalog, it is not, by any practical definition, e-procurement, and for companies with more than a few suppliers (imagine doing this with 50,000 suppliers), the approach hardly seems viable.

As these e-markets have become more popular, however, significant progress has been made—using new XML-based standards (see Chapter 7)—toward making it possible for buyers' ERP systems to accept some types of straightforward documents, such as purchase orders or receipts. But because the procurement process involves many other types of interaction—discounts, contract terms, buying, shipping and receiving arrangements—until greater levels of interoperability are available and more consistent communications protocol standards are agreed upon, much of the process will remain little more than an electronically enhanced paper-based system.

Many would also argue that although this type of Internet-based procurement makes it easier for employees to buy ORM materials, that same ease of use could easily invite abuse, with employees circumventing company purchasing policies and freely purchasing from any online vendor. At a time when maverick buying is seen as an area of cost concern, this type of setup seems only really appropriate for small buyers and one-off purchases.

BUY-SIDE ONE-TO-MANY MODEL

In the buy-side one-to-many model (shown in Figure 6.2), the buyer maintains in-house the catalogs and databases of multiple suppliers' goods and services, and is responsible for tying all transactions into the company's purchasing and financial systems. Although the vendors (sellers) provide catalogue information on products, services, prices, availability, and so on, the buyer, as host, is responsible for keeping that information up to date. Most systems will then tie the purchase order to an electronic invoice, providing for simultaneous settlement through electronic funds transfer, and through the ERP system, will automate the workflow and approval processes. All of this is integrated into the desktop-based requisition system.

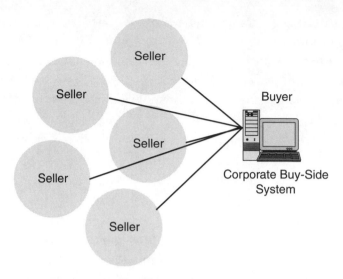

Figure 6.2 Buy–side one–to–many model.

It has the advantage of ease of use, and because many of the large ERP vendors are adding this functionality to their product suites, can theoretically provide easier and closer ties to internal ERP systems.

The obvious advantages of the buyer-managed arrangement are that it allows the purchasing department to control the products and services available on the catalogs and can tie systems—such as procurement cards—directly to employees, setting quantity limits, pricing ceilings, and other criteria. This has been, until recently, the favored model when attempting to bring the self-service desktop model to employees.

The buyer-managed model requires, by its nature, a good deal of buyer-vendor negotiation and collaboration, because the buyer has taken on the responsibility for maintaining current descriptions of products, availability, lead times for delivery, and prices. In fact, despite the current popularity of the online exchanges and subscription-based third-party e-markets, this buyer-managed model still has many proponents. It is a model that has worked well in the past for very large customers and for groups of customers and suppliers that have a long-term relationship or a natural affinity to a certain buyer-seller market.

Within this buy-side model, there are two different areas of focus: buy-side desktop requisitioning and buy-side Internet-based central procurement.

Buy-Side Desktop Requisitioning

This set of software resides both on a company's intranet and on users' desktop PCs, and allows employees to purchase items directly from their desks using preapproved catalogs. Although employees are given the freedom to purchase goods when they need them, managerial control remains with purchasing professionals, and there is a full audit trail. Guidelines, discounts, prices, contracts, and approval levels are controlled by procurement management.

A typical example is Visio, a developer of engineering and drawing software, who selected Concur Procurement, Concur Technologies' Internet-based desktop requisitioning software, as the platform for an indirect materials e-procurement initiative. The system provides employees with the ability to order materials and track their delivery directly from their desktop PCs, with an electronic approval tree and well-defined order limits. Visio reports that it saved some $500,000 in the first year, with an ROI of less than four months.

Supporters of these desktop requisitioning systems cite the value of "off loading" the purchase of day-to-day indirect ORM items from busy specialists in the purchasing department, and claim that desktop requisitioning greatly reduces maverick buying, forcing employees to purchase indirect goods using prearranged purchase agreements, and providing for a much more accurate record and audit trail of indirect spending.

Buy-Side Central Procurement

Increasingly powerful in terms of their performance measurement and decision support capabilities, the major buy-side applications allow purchasing professionals (central purchasing) to set parameters, develop contracts, analyze supplier performance, measure transaction costs, and understand total *true cost* of procurement. Although intended for indirect purchasing, increasingly, buy-side applications are being adapted for bulk or standardized purchase of direct goods.

The greatest drawback to these buyer-managed systems (excluding those who outsource to ASPs) remains the laborious task of catalog and system maintenance. Buyer-managed catalogs allow you to store catalog data on your own premises, with electronic updates periodically sent across the Internet by the supplier. But there is significant effort required in the initial aggregation and rationalization process. In fact, the process is ongoing, and because many large firms deal with hundreds or even thousands of suppliers in different countries, there may be thousands of items that each have multiple specifications. Different suppliers have different terms for similar products, and various suppliers will provide images in different formats, with inconsistent product ID numbers. Accordingly, for those companies who don't necessarily see catalog and systems maintenance as a core competency, outsourcing of these tasks seems an appealing option.

It is also possible, of course, to outsource the design and maintenance of product catalogs to teams of information engineers who can organize and standardize your product catalogs for you. Companies such as Requisite Technology provide both a service and a software suite (which includes a powerful data search engine) that will help standardize the wide variety of product information of multiple suppliers, and includes the ability to scan paper catalogs.

Even if you decide to outsource these content maintenance and aggregation activities, your systems will need to provide for at least three different methods of maintenance access in order to provide for flexibility of policy in the future. The system will need to provide for Web-based maintenance so that suppliers can update their own catalogs, so that you can update the catalogs yourself, or so that you can pay a third party to maintain the catalogs for you. It is important to remember that ASPs vary widely in terms of their support for these catalog maintenance technologies.

INDEPENDENT PORTAL AND ONLINE TRADING COMMUNITIES

It may well be that the development of the independent portal site (shown in Figure 6.3)—where multiple buyers and sellers can meet electronically and transact all types of business through a single point of integration—will be one of the most significant events, both in terms of IT and economic development, since the invention of the microchip. The portal model, a single Web site entry point available to anyone on the Internet, worldwide, allows any participant to log on and transact business for a subscription fee, a transaction charge, or a percentage of exchange fee. Activities include viewing catalogs, placing orders (or bidding, in the case of online auctions), and routing payments.

It is probably not hyperbole to say that seldom in history has so much money and attention been focused so intensively on a single new growth area in the economy (see Figure 6.4). To illustrate the point, consider that in the spring of 1999, there were around 30 ver-

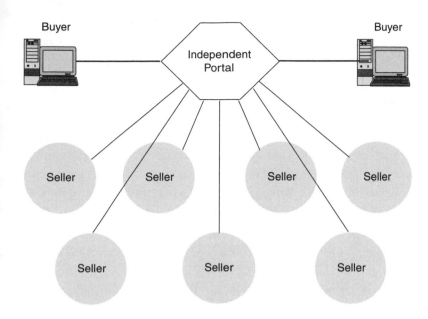

Figure 6.3 Independent portal model.

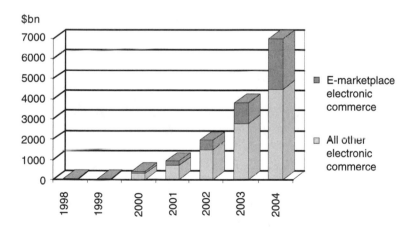

Figure 6.4 B2B e-commerce forecast. (Source: The Gartner Group as printed in "FT-IT Review 2," *The Financial Times,* October 18, 2000.)

tical e-marketplaces online. By the end of 2000, that number was approaching 1,500. There are today representatives from every conceivable support area of procurement and supply chain—software vendors, hardware suppliers, venture capitalists, and industry-leading organizations from vertical industries—that moved quickly to form collaborations with other interested parties in order to sponsor industry-focused electronic trading communities. Some analysts, alarmed at the enormous amount of activity in this area, estimate that there may be as many as 10,000 e-marketplace trading communities by 2003. Volpe Brown Whelan & Co. estimates that e-marketplaces will account for $35 billion in transactions by 2004.[1]

The sponsors for these electronic trading hubs also vary in ambition and levels of service. Taking their inspiration from companies such as Amazon.com and eBay, many exchanges are limited to providing an online many-to-many storefront for multiple buyers and suppliers, usually focused on a single horizontal or vertical industry sector. In truth, in these early days, most e-markets are primarily focused on selling indirect goods often via auctions and a "spot market," which currently accounts for between 10% and 30% of procurement being carried out over trading hubs today.

VERTICAL E-MARKETS AND MARKETPLACE CREATORS

E-market exchanges and electronic trading communities tend to be focused on either vertical or horizontal markets, so it might be worth looking at the distinction between the two. Vertical market trading communities tend to focus on one particular industry—steel, paper, electricity, paper, chemicals, home loans—and are usually sponsored, or at least supported, by one or several of the leading companies in that area.

There are hundreds of examples of vertical markets. The chemical industry, for example, has shown early leadership in developing online marketplaces, with more than 50 announced e-markets, which range from simple online auctions to complex virtual distributorships that service entire continents. They have an advantage over other vertical industries in that chemicals for the most part adhere to well-accepted international standards in terms of naming, quality, content, and quantities, thereby making online auction-type purchasing—where the buyer may have no personal contact with the seller and therefore must be certain of exactly what is being purchased—easier. Other vertical industry areas that have rushed to develop e-marketplaces include automotive, energy, high-tech manufacturing and electronics, communications, publishing, metals, aerospace, financial services, healthcare, and many more (see Figure 6.5).

An interesting phenomenon has occurred in this area that has surprised many industry watchers and analysts. A testament to the radical changes that the Internet can bring about, many of these vertical e-market trading communities are now being sponsored jointly and collaboratively by large and powerful industry leaders. Often long-time rivals, these *market creators,* as they have become known, have—by virtue of their industry experience, extensive business connections, and financial clout—quickly risen to critical mass to become the dominant leaders within the vertical industry electronic marketplace.

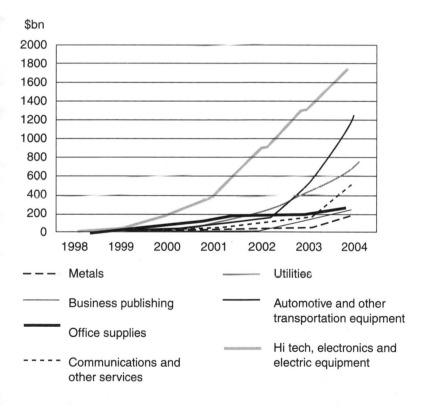

Figure 6.5 B2B e-commerce forecast by industry. (Source: The Gartner Group as printed in "Electronic Trading Is Expected to Surge," *The Financial Times,* October 18, 2000.)

The Covisint alliance between Ford, General Motors, Daimler-Chrysler, and Renault-Nissan is probably the most famous example. This massively powerful collaboration involves 750,000 tier-three and tier-four suppliers, 50,000 tier two suppliers, and 1,500 tier one suppliers, all tied to 14 vehicle manufacturers. As a reflection of the influence and power of this group, in return for installing the robust and sophisticated procurement platform, Commerce One will be paid not only a good amount of cash, but will also collect a portion of Covisint's gross revenues for 10 years, and get a 2% equity stake in the venture. In return, GM and Ford will share an equity stake in Commerce One worth $1.23 billion.[2]

In high-tech manufacturing, a group of 12 important industry leaders, including Hewlett-Packard, Compaq, NEC, Gateway, Hitachi, Samsung, and others, have joined together to form an electronic trading community that will focus on the estimated $600 billion high-tech components and parts market, and will offer open sourcing, auctions, and supply planning and logistics support.

In chemicals, giants such as British Petroleum, Dow, Shell, BASF, Bayer, and DuPont have formed an online chemical trading community that provides for exchange of virtually any chemical-related item, from broad procurement to key product areas such as plastics and laboratory chemicals. There are announced sites for agrochemicals, bulk chemicals, and custom-made chemicals, for shipping and logistics services, for trade of excess inventory, and for special geographical areas such as China, India, Singapore, and Europe. And although trading volume is still comparatively small, online transactions are growing rapidly, and these exchanges are already beginning to link with other online markets—such as automotive and aerospace—with which they share a large number of customers.

The retail industry has seen a similar scramble among long-time competitors to create consortium-sponsored exchanges. Sears joined up with France's Carrefour and five equity partners to set up Global-NetXchange, and were quickly challenged by the WorldWide Retail Exchange, made up of 11 other prominent international retail firms, including Safeway, Target, Kmart and CVS from the U.S., Tesco and Marks & Spencers from the U.K., and Casino from France. Over 1,000 suppliers have been invited to join in the exchange, and although in real terms trade online is still very small, both groups have announced plans to provide members with services that include collaborative planning, supply chain, and logistics services. Similarly, giants such as Georgia Pacific, International Paper, and Weyerhauser have allied to form an exchange that is focused on the paper industry.

There are also any number of cross-industry alliances developing. DuPont, Cargill and Cenex Harvest are putting together Rooster.com as a vertical exchange to provide seed and equipment to farmers and to help them sell their crops online. Even professional services companies such as PriceWaterhouseCoopers have launched a B2B marketplace consortium that provides an exchange for purchase of ORM goods and services.

These enormously powerful industry coalitions—and there are already more than 60—have essentially overwhelmed the online marketplace industry, driving smaller sites out of business and making viable exchanges pause in their development, waiting to see where the intervention of these large market creators will take their particular industries.

In many ways, these vertical industry e-markets have an advantage over the horizontal or cross-industry trading exchanges, in that the sponsors, as both buyers and (if manufacturers) sellers themselves, will tend to reap a huge benefit from the efficient provision of supplies to their industry. Many industry watchers contend that vertical industry online exchanges, based on their combination of industry knowledge and collaborative organization, don't even need to make a profit in order for all participants to benefit.

In fact, the threat of future antitrust legislation still looms over these large consortium electronic markets. The idea of long-time competitors sharing not only part-ownership in an enterprise, but also sharing pricing and supply information, to many sounds off alarm bells in terms of price fixing bias and antitrust dangers.

HORIZONTAL E-MARKETS

Horizontal trading communities, on the other hand, cut across the boundaries of industries and focus on broad categories of goods— office supplies, furniture, travel services, janitorial help—that are common to large numbers of cross-industry organizations. Horizontal e-markets are often sponsored by e-procurement software groups or leaders in specific areas of these types of indirect goods and service provision. Horizontal exchanges have, at least in the past, been driven primarily by indirect materials and tend to develop in highly fragmented markets.

W.W. Grainger, the powerful MRO supplies group, provides a perfect example of the horizontal trading community. Their exchange, OrderZone.com, went online in May 1999, and provides a single Web portal that gives customers access to six industry-leading MRO suppliers. The service includes online ordering and invoicing and provides customers with a single point of contact for access to a wide variety of indirect products. Only one registration on this single Web site is necessary to gain access to not only Grainger.com and its MRO catalogs, but to catalogs of other leading indirect suppliers for items such as office and computer supplies, laboratory equipment, and uniforms.

Some would also contend that companies such as Ariba and Commerce One are in fact not only software providers, but horizontal exchanges as well, in that they provide a trading community for a broad spectrum of suppliers of ORM and MRO materials, regardless of vertical industry. For example, Office Depot has aligned with Commerce One's MarketSite to provide an online trading community for their ORM goods in the U.S., the U.K., and Japan. Ariba has purchased SupplierMarket.com, which is an online marketplace for manufacturing materials. The fact that various vertical industry exchanges have begun to use their software and exchange networks means that the lines between vertical and horizontal markets are blurred even farther.

There are a number of variations on this central theme, but basically all of these groups—whether known as trading hubs, exchanges, or e-markets—are focused on creating a global electronic hub based upon their single, industry-focused portal, which will provide seamless integration through the entire supply chain, allowing buyers and suppliers of every size and type, and from any country, to transact all their business through a single electronic marketplace. Supported by a broad mix of hardware, software, communications, and industry specialist companies, they differ significantly—in focus, size, level of service, and market—and range from enormously powerful collaborations between automakers to tiny e-marketplace hubs for buying specialty products, such as motorboat equipment or wine.

W.W. GRAINGER AND BFGOODRICH

In business since 1927, W.W. Grainger, Inc. has a number of Web properties, but Grainger.com is the granddaddy of them all (in terms of sales as well as time on the Net). In 1999, Grainger had $4.5 billion in sales, with more than $100 million over the Web, the majority of which was placed through Grainger.com.

More than 560,000 brand name maintenance, repair, and operating (MRO) supplies are offered at Grainger.com, with a growing number of Grainger's 1.5 million customers actively ordering online. The Web site continues the same kind of customer service and wide range of industrial products provided in the traditional business, with the additional convenience of 24/7 ordering.

This convenience is what first hooked Isaac Pendarvis, assistant buyer for BFGoodrich Aerospace in Pueblo, Colorado. As Pendarvis says, "I'd known about Grainger since I was a kid, so one day I was on the Internet and tried out their site and was hooked. It's one of the most convenient and easy sites to use."

Pendarvis makes purchases for the entire BFGoodrich plant of approximately 250 employees. He used to call in orders to suppliers, give the salesperson a part number, and wait until the price could be pulled up. There was also the chance that numbers could be transposed. Now he can place orders online in a matter of minutes, and his display has BFGoodrich's

pricing built in. Pendarvis can get just about anything he needs from Grainger.com. [interface with other supplie...] says, "so if I need something specific that they don't normally carry, they'll research and find the items through their FindMRO.com site, and with their buying power, they can get better prices than I can, so I save money as well as time."

BFGoodrich has achieved additional savings from the tremendous decrease in paperwork. Individuals in each department now have access to purchasing cards (P-cards), which allow them to do some of their own ordering. "Before, we had to issue purchase orders for every little thing," says Pendarvis, "but now employees with P-cards and passwords can place orders according to the spending limits that have been set up for their positions."

Last year, the BFGoodrich Pueblo operation made $100,000 in purchases from Grainger.com, which reflects a 10 to 15 percent savings. BFGoodrich has now signed a companywide enterprise agreement that allows every BFGoodrich facility in the country to order through Grainger.com, with an expected savings of at least 10 percent....

Source: "E-Procurement: Unleashing Corporate Purchasing Power," ©2001 Time Inc., all rights reserved. www.fortune.com/sections/eprocurement2000, retrieved July 19, 2000.

In fact, a good deal of criticism has been leveled already at some of these exchanges—both large and small—because it is alleged that they are simply industry leaders who, although experts in the provision of goods and services to their own markets, understand little about technology or the complex interaction of software and new business processes over the Internet. Accordingly, almost every trading hub and exchange is moving toward becoming a consortium of various ASPs, software vendors, and other third-party support organizations. Many e-marketplaces are in fact now run by ASPs.

All of these types of trading hubs typically make their money by charging a 1% to 15% fee for each transaction, depending on volume and materials being sold. Even then, the buyer usually comes out well ahead—often saving up to 40% on the price they would have paid through their traditional distribution channels.[3]

AUCTIONS

A subset of these online trading communities is the online auction, which provides an online, real-time exchange for commodities in a particular vertical or horizontal industry—office supplies, auto parts, chemicals—with prospective buyers and sellers logging on and making some type of low-price offer against a request. The buyer then makes an online purchase from the vendor who provides an offer that best meets his or her needs. Some sites provide essentially a commodity market, with sellers posting their goods and prices and buyers logging on looking for bargains. Others are initiated by buyers making their needs known, with suppliers responding—bidding against other suppliers in real-time—to make a best offer. These sites can involve participants from all over the world, and most auctions are completed within an allotted amount of time—say an hour—giving suppliers time to move toward a natural floor-level price, and as in all markets, with a flurry of activity to get in before the bell. The result is actually most often a "reverse auction," where the price goes down, not up, as the bidding progresses.

Many of these e-market auction sites provide the software to generate the purchase order and exchange invoicing information, and provide at least some level of order tracking and delivery coordination. Others have gone even farther, providing tendering services—usually in the form of a Request For Tender (RFT)—rather than simple commodity auctions. In fact, the better online auction e-markets offer several important services beyond just providing the electronic, real-time negotiations between buyer and seller. These include easy-to-understand classification of RFTs, proactive electronic notification of upcoming auctions by category, calendars and scheduled times for important auctions, and even prequalification of likely suppliers on behalf of the buyer.

This type of real-time bidding is most appropriate for high-volume, generic, commodity-type goods, where small differences in price on large volumes add up quickly. As you might expect, online auctions are usually focused on indirect goods, although they too are beginning be seen as providing an instant online spot market for direct materials—particularly if supplies of those materials are known and predictable. Some sites, like Free Trade Zone, are a combination of ASPs and e-marketplace, providing not only an online auction service, but also helping bring vendors that can supply difficult-to-find components to manufacturers. This is the type of service that will help e-markets move from indirect goods to MRO and direct materials in the future.

The cost of these auctions to participants varies widely. Most charge a straightforward fee based upon either transactions or on a percentage of the dollar value of the trade. SupplierMarket.com, for example, an auction that matches buyers and suppliers for build-to-order manufacturing contracts, charges a transaction fee averaging 2% of the total bid.[4] SciQuest, an online exchange for scientific supplies, takes a different approach. They began by offering premium placement for suppliers on a first come, first served basis. As they became more viable, they were then able to charge new suppliers an additional fee—some 400 vendors have paid from $2,000 to $15,000 for advantageous positioning on the site. This is on top of a standard supplier fee of some 8% to 10% commission per order.[5]

There are two key advantages to the online auction: speed and cost reduction.

1. **Speed.** For anyone who has ever had to go through the cumbersome process of sending out or responding to RFPs, the value of the online approach is obvious. Instead of taking several months to receive and evaluate supplier responses, the entire process can be completed in little more than an hour. Today when companies send out RFPs, it can take weeks and sometimes months to evaluate all the bids and negotiate the final deal. Because the bidders do the negotiating, real-time, online auctions can reduce that time to 90 minutes.

AUCTIONS

Bruce Platzman was intrigued but wary when he first heard about SupplierMarket.com's Internet marketplace for buyers and sellers of manufactured direct materials. Platzman, CEO of Affordable Interior Systems (QIS), Inc., of Hudson, Massachusetts, a major manufacturer of office systems and workstations, liked the idea of going online to procure direct materials. "It sounded cutting-edge and exciting," he says, "but I also was skeptical. I always try to balance upside potential against risk."

No matter how he analyzed it, however, Platzman couldn't find any risk. The Burlington, Massachusetts-based marketplace provider charged no up-front fees for software installation or consulting services, and using the service required no technology beyond an Internet connection and a standard browser.

Platzman's procurement team pulled together a request for quotes (RFQ) for a year's supply of three-millimeter banding, the protective plastic molding that fits around the edges of office furniture. They did that using SupplierMarket.com's forms-based RFQ Builder facility, which guides purchasers step by step through the creation of an RFQ, complete with drawings. At that point, behind the scenes, SupplierMarket.com's SmartMatch technology automatically matched registered qualified suppliers with the RFQ, based on their technical and commercial capabilities. Those suppliers were then invited to participate in a live online auction.

A couple of weeks later, Platzman was working in his office and keeping one eye on his computer screen, watching companies place bids for his order. Suddenly the online action had his full attention. Six more suppliers had jumped into the bidding and the price had already dropped below his expectations. He called in other members of the company's management team and they all watched in amazement as the price continued to fall. By the time the bidding was over, a little more than two hours after it had started, Affordable Interiors was looking at a low bid of $102,000 for an item that typically cost around $170,000.

Euphoria quickly gave way to doubt. "When you look at a number like that, you have to ask yourself, 'Who the heck bid this thing? Is it some guy working out of his garage?' says Platzman. As it turned out, the bidder was no garage operation. It was the premier manufacturer of the required type of plastic edging, a company that regularly supplied Affordable Interior's largest competitors. "We landed with what we believe is not only the largest, but the highest-quality manufacturer of this product," says Platzman, who was so happy with that outcome that he has since posted 12 more RFQs.

REVERSE AUCTIONS

Reverse auctions—where suppliers bid prices down to win contracts—are hot in B2B e-commerce. And Web sites where buying organizations can hold such auctions are springing up rapidly.

Since 1997, Quaker Oats has saved $8.5 million by purchasing via reverse online auctions, according to Carl Curry, vice president of integrated purchasing and logistics. And SmithKline Beecham, a pharmaceutical and consumer healthcare company, recently announced $3 million in savings through online auctions.

Both companies chose to conduct auctions at FreeMarkets Inc. (freemarkets.com). Other Web sites where buyers can hold reverse auctions include SupplierMarket.com, BidtheWorld.com, frpMarket.com, and eBreviate.com.

Curry says Quaker Oats first heard about online reverse auctions about three years ago when a senior member of his department encountered a FreeMarkets representative at the Center for Advanced Purchasing Studies in Arizona.

"At that point FreeMarkets was talking about the concept in terms of what they intended to deliver and how their system was going to work," says Curry. "[Our person] came back excited, saying 'Boy if this becomes functional we ought to be an early player.'"

From there, Curry and the rest of his department started looking for commodity contracts that were coming up for renewal, which the company could put out for bid on the FreeMarkets Web site. Glycerin was the first product they put out to bid. Since then the company has held regular auctions on the site, reaping large savings. Curry says the $8.5 million represents the amount of savings the company achieved versus prices it had in place before going to FreeMarkets.

The process for conducting a reverse auction on the FreeMarkets site begins with choosing which contracts will be put out for bid, Curry says. After that, a supplier evaluation process begins where the buying company looks at its list of suppliers to decide which ones will be offered a chance to bid for the contract. At that point, FreeMarkets also searches its own list for qualified suppliers.

"FreeMarkets typically brings back their list, which may differ somewhat from our own. They may have experience with suppliers with whom we haven't worked or they may be more global," says Curry. "We canvas the list of suppliers to determine if they can meet our initial needs from a quality and response perspective."

The next step, Curry says, is to write the RFQ and send it out via email to all qualified suppliers along with information as to when the bidding will take place.

After that, the buying company uses its Web browser to click into the Web site and watch the bidding. "The auctions generally take place in about 20 to 30 minutes," Curry says. "Then we determine who won the bid and award the contract from there."

Source: "e-Procurement Strategies: Big Buyers Jump on the Net," *Purchasing Online,* March 23, 2000, pp. 8–9.

2. **Cost reduction.** Obviously, for buyers, this type of online approach helps to cut the administrative costs of dealing with thousands of small companies. Auctions also tend to drive the price of goods down significantly, partly because the nature of real-time spot-buying itself quickly pushes prices downward, and partly because the certainty of immediate sale and contract acceptance means that the normal mark-up that the seller includes in their prices for covering risk can be eliminated. For sellers, the online auction greatly expands their potential customer base, allowing vendors an opportunity to quickly and dynamically price and move materials.

There are already many converts. United Technologies, for example, began an online, in-house auction that it has used since 1997 for commodity products—electronic components, motors, wire and plastic parts—which account for nearly 25% of the $14 billion that the company spends each year on these types of indirect and MRO goods.[6] Quaker Oats claims to have saved some $8.5 million using its own email-based auction system.

SmithKline Beecham, a pharmaceutical and consumer health-care group, recently announced $3 million in savings through online auctions. The company has been using the FreeMarkets.com auction site since 1999 and has purchased more than $38.2 million worth of goods and services online. SmithKline Beecham reports it has cut overall price of goods by nearly 10%. The FreeMarkets auction site says it has facilitated more than $575 million worth of bids for indirect goods and services, saving an average of 13% for its Global 1000 clients. FreeMarkets deals with some 46 different types of indirect goods and services, from MRO items to tax preparation services and car rentals.[7]

Although the benefits are obvious, auctions have their drawbacks too. For one thing, at this time at least, they remain primarily focused on spot market buying of indirect goods. Although there is no doubt that the process drives prices down and greatly reduces administrative time and costs, the entire focus also works against some of the key principles of procurement. It is difficult to predict prices, for example, as each day may bring a completely different set of bid responses.

More important, and something that has been increasingly annoying to suppliers, the focus on real-time pricing undermines the added-value nature that differentiates one supplier from another. *Many economists argue that the transparent nature of auctions, and the myopic focus on price, essentially eliminates any concept of competitive advantage.* In fact, because the emphasis of an auction is on price alone, it makes it difficult for suppliers to maintain any close relationship with the buyer, and yet issues concerning collaborative part design, quality assurance levels, and delivery dependability, are often much more important in procurement of MRO or direct goods, particularly, than price alone.

APPLICATION SERVICE PROVIDERS

ASPs are third-party service organizations that provide hosted applications that service either a one-to-many buyer model or a many-to-many industry trading community. With the advantage of maintaining all the software, catalogs, and store files on their own servers, they provide an opportunity for companies—both buyers and sellers—to participate in electronic trading communities without having to buy, install, or maintain their own software. They provide essential e-procurement services, such as catalog content aggregation and maintenance, electronic requisitioning, contract development, order and delivery management, and electronic payment, and can process transactions using various forms of EDI, XML, and other communications protocols. All of this is provided for a license fee, a subscription, or for various forms of usage charges.

ASPs came about in the past few years because, as we have seen, the early e-procurement solutions based on the buyer-managed model required significant time, effort, and resources by both buyers and sellers in order to maintain catalogs, systems, and multiple forms of communications protocols. There was a ready market for third-parties that could provide those services as core competency and remove that burden from the buyers and sellers, who were more interested in the business transaction itself than in maintaining catalogs or systems support.

Although they have had some success with the largest companies, their appeal, at least in these first formative years, has been particularly to small and mid-sized companies, which had neither the internal content management and IT resources nor the cash to buy, implement, and maintain complex and expensive e-procurement applications internally. ASPs provide companies with a cost-effective method for buying into a scaleable solution that they might not normally be able to afford.

vever, when it became obvious that there was a significant for this type of service (see Figure 6.6), others began to move ᵉ third-party hosting arena, differentiating themselves by ; an increasing number of valuable business services to ᵃany the basic service of the buyer-seller portal site. Some-ᵗnown as Enterprise Asset Management (EAM), not only did ᵉervice providers offer catalog maintenance and basic order and payment transactions services, but they also now provide various types of supply chain management, inventory replenishment, directory services and routing, transportation, CRM, order tracking services, and even fulfillment insurance. Some even provide integration with travel services and 401(k) processing.

A good example of software platforms themselves providing these services can be seen with Intelisys Electronic Commerce (now Metiom) and its support of the Autolink.com e-market. Because many of the smaller auto suppliers that want to participate have little IT or content management experience, Intelisys built, and as Metiom, now manages the site, maintaining both the database and server, and providing catalogs, management tools, and links to other industry suppliers. A similar service is provided by Essential Markets.com, which offers a hosted service that helps small suppliers to convert their product information into XML formats, and then places those supplier details on the Internet, including links to e-marketplaces.

Similarly, M2MEport.com, which is targeted to small and medium-sized manufacturers, provides not only an e-market portal, but also a consultative "Collaboration Center," where their specialists work with subscribers in the design of customized products. They have even gone so far as to provide a variety of education offerings—

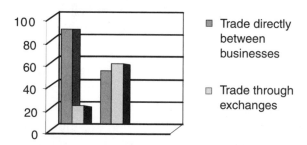

Figure 6.6 Intermediation: B2B e-commerce, percent of total. (Source: Forrester Research as printed in "Seller Beware," *The Economist,* March 4, 2000.)

including a distance learning program—designed to help manufacturers with procurement-related issues. Others, like Grainger.com, provide access to important technical support information and material safety data sheets for products sold through their Order-Zone.com site.

Recognizing the potential for ASP outsourcing, and as a further twist to this convoluted marketplace, Clarus, Microsoft, and Cisco Systems have agreed to collaborate with a selected group of ASPs to provide them with hosted services that are designed for use by ASPs, and that incorporate ASP-specific tools that will make it easier for these ASPs to deliver e-procurement services on an outsourced basis to their customers. This reflects the high level of competition in this marketplace, and the fact that in order to survive, ASPs have been forced to seek out multiple revenue streams, including leasing applications and even building portals themselves.

THE FUTURE OF E-MARKETS

In fact, so popular and lucrative has the entire market become that there has arisen a number of third-party vendors that specialize in building and operating e-markets, boasting that a basic trading hub can be set up in three to six weeks for a few hundred thousand dollars. This has meant that many people with an entrepreneurial flair and a good working knowledge of a vertical industry supply chain have been tempted to plunge into the market with their own trading hub. Venture capitalists, understanding the popularity and the potential "winner-take-all" scenario for those entering these e-marketplaces, have been only too keen to provide the funding.

There are drawbacks, of course. As with any independent many-to-many portal at this time, both suppliers and buyers still have to update their internal systems manually with each transaction. Although obviously the trend is toward full integration, there are currently any number of differences—in buying parameters, payment systems, shipping and delivery techniques—that mean that purchasing through an e-market is still not much different (at least in terms of process efficiencies) from negotiating price over the telephone. This leaves the "e-market revolution" much less revolutionary than its proponents claim, in that neither the buyer nor the seller are fundamentally changing anything about their businesses.

However, many industry watchers and software vendors would counter that it is only a matter of time before that higher level of integration is provided by the e-market portal owners. In fact, this need has already been partly addressed by a whole new platform of third-party integration software known as *connectors* (see "Translation and Connectivity" in Chapter 5).

Many of the early exchanges and auctions that focused on spot markets found that they were soon overtaken by larger, better-funded trading communities sponsored by alliances between market creators and the large software companies. Moreover, many of the smaller auction sites have found that contractual details and performance guarantees, necessary to ensure that buyers won't get burned badly by participating, require software and processes that incorporate a sophisticated and detailed approach to automated bidding—levels of expertise that they do not have and software that very few of them can either build themselves or afford to buy.

But of all the controversial issues that this revolutionary shift toward trading hubs raises, one of the most important is that it runs completely counter to the prevailing wisdom—that has been gaining momentum over the past decade—of the value of strategic sourcing. The idea behind strategic sourcing is that a few, preselected, tested, and trusted vendor partnerships are far more cost-effective—because of familiarity with processes and expectations, negotiated discounts, and ability to be trusted with secure information—than many partnerships with unknown or untested vendors, even if they are offering one-off low prices for their goods. Dedication to this premise is, according to many, the very reason why companies want and need to digitize their procurement systems, in that once their procurement specialists are no longer laboring with low-cost, high-volume indirect goods, they can spend their time much more valuably in developing closer, tightly-negotiated arrangements with a few highly-trusted partners.

Over the past several years, for example, IBM has significantly reduced the number of vendors from which they purchase ORM materials. In Europe, only 10 suppliers provide the company with some three-quarters of all of its purchases. But this vendor rationalization is not as straightforward as it might appear. The ultimate number of suppliers may well be what it was before consolidation. It is simply that IBM has, because of its considerable market leverage, been able to force the costly and cumbersome responsibility for negotiating and buying from thousands of suppliers down one level to its selected and trusted "clearinghouse"-type partners. It is a form of strategic sourcing, but not one that is easily adopted by smaller, less influential buyers.

On the other hand, many procurement specialists—both buyers and sellers—assert that spot markets, auctions, and many-to-many exchanges completely undermine the trusted one-to-one relationship that is at the heart of the strategic sourcing movement. On the contrary, at least until these e-market portals can be closely and securely integrated with a buying company's ERP and back-end systems, item price becomes the single most important criteria for trading with a particular vendor, which may be one of thousands of suppliers, each one selling on multiple horizontal and vertical industry e-markets. It is an unexpected strategic paradox that promises to divide the procurement community.

In the end, of course, it is the very fears expressed by industry watchers that a single e-marketplace will become dominant (winner take all) that are part of the motivation for venture capitalists to risk money backing a myriad of these e-marketplace startups. So volatile is this portion of the economy that there is some merit in spreading your risk. *But there can be little doubt that the vast majority of startup exchanges will rapidly collapse as they are tested in the rough-and-tumble of the day-to-day procurement market.* Customers will increasingly demand higher levels of service and integrated functionality from trading hubs, forcing a form of natural selection to take place in each industry vertical.

Much in the same way, there is also little doubt that customer demand, legal barriers permitting, will soon force these multiple and competing groups—e-procurement software vendors, ERP firms, market creators, auctions, exchanges, ASPs—toward consolidation. Customers are already demonstrating that they don't want to have to deal with a myriad of different vertical and horizontal suppliers. They want one or two organizations that can provide centralized sourcing for them. Many research groups contend that the need for a single, integrated solution for the full e-procurement process—for both indirect and direct materials and with an acceptable balance of systems integration capability and security—will quickly force a consolidation of the now fragmented e-procurement marketplace.

No longer able to focus on simply providing buyers with purchasing leverage and sellers with a broader market, those that survive, claim analysts, are being forced to add value by offering supply chain management expertise, back-end systems integration, integrated banking, and data security protection, all in a single, cost-effective offering. This will mean that when market forces take their course, according to the Gartner Group, there will only be room for about three vertical portals in each industry. The others will go the way of the e-commerce dotcom startups of the past several years.

There is already evidence that that vertical industry shakeout has begun. One good example is EFDEX, the e-market that had hoped to become the dominant exchange in the catering industry, bringing together online restaurants and hotels with catering suppliers for food and drink. At one point, their staff had jumped from 20 to 200, but in the end, investor concerns about cost and the site's ability to attract the number of users necessary meant that EFDEX failed to secure the necessary funding to even go live.

Similarly, IndustrialVortex, the industrial automation product e-exchange, collapsed after only six months of trading, despite more than $20 million in RFQs processed in a single month in the summer of 2000. Neoforma, a highly praised health care exchange, was forced to lay off 25% of its workforce, its stock price dropping from $60 to $3.50.[8]

Most spectacularly, Ventro, which operates many different marketplaces, was forced to close two of its once most promising vertical exchanges. Chemdex, a market site for medical products, and Promedix, which provided an exchange for specialty medical products, were both at one time cited as sterling examples of the promise of vertical markets, but ultimately failed to attract enough participants or make enough money to survive.

It may well be that if only as a matter of survival, as some argue, e-markets will move quickly to build in the third-party delivery and quality assurance services necessary to reassure buyers. The larger and more progressive trading communities—and this is where things become potentially revolutionary—are already providing a marketplace for direct materials, creating a much closer integration of supply chain systems than could have been contemplated only two years ago. There are many reasons for this, not least that the potential earnings are so good that the e-procurement and ERP software groups are scrambling to reshape themselves as partners in these hubs and exchanges, and are bringing valuable procurement expertise to add on to the features of the industry focus.

The reason that these types of Internet-based markets are so important, then, is that they may well be the catalyst that will push e-procurement away from the limited one-to-many extranet model, focused on a single buyer and several preferred vendors, toward a many-to-many arrangement where, even for many direct materials, buyers will go to a single online portal in order to bid on materials being sold on a real-time market.

ENDNOTES

1. Girishankar, Saroja, "New Options Fuel Growth in Online Procurement," *Information Week,* www.informationweek.com, January 10, 2000, p. 2–4; "E-Procurement: Unleashing Corporate Purchasing Power," ©2001 Time Inc., all rights reserved. www.fortune.com/sections/eprocurement2000, retrieved July 19, 2000.
2. "Commerce One and Covisint Strike Deal," *The Financial Times,* December 13, 2000.
3. Girishankar, Saroja, "New Options Fuel Growth in Online Procurement," *Information Week,* www.informationweek.com, January 10, 2000, p. 2.
4. Wilder, Clinton, "Industrial Procurement: Online Options Grow," *Informationweek Online,* October 18, 1999, p. 1.
5. Knorr, Dick, "Dawn of the Digital Marketplace," *Upside Today,* October 26, 1999, p. 6.
6. Marsh, Peter, "Virtual Auctions Knock Down Costs," *The Financial Times,* March 11, 1998, p. 18.
7. "E-Procurement Strategies: Big Buyers Jump on the Internet," *Purchasing Online,* March 23, 2000, pp. 8–9.
8. Wilson, Tim, "Exchanges on the Edge," *Internetweek Online,* August 11, 2000, p. 1.

7 Standards

Objective

The development of new communications standards that allow buyers and sellers to transmit important purchasing transaction data easily and securely has been a critical element in the successful development of e-procurement systems:

- Because the effectiveness of any e-procurement or integrated order fulfillment system is dependent upon passing purchasing data from system to system, agreement on industry standards for communications has become of paramount importance.

- XML (Extensible Markup Language) promises to provide a simple and affordable solution for secure exchange of transactional business data between firms.

- XML standards are being set by various bodies and tend to be different in their development, based upon major industry sectors.

As with every movement in the information technology arena over the past 45 years, the need for interoperability between competing hardware and software plat-

It is safe to say that any company that can afford to have an EDI link probably already has it. In fact, only 300,000 firms worldwide have ever adopted EDI.

forms means that agreement on industry standards for communications has become of paramount importance. But unlike most media (email, video, etc.) carried over the Internet today, business documents have traditionally lacked agreed standards, particularly with regard to ordering and invoicing information. It is safe to say that any company that can afford to have an EDI link probably already has it. In fact, only 300,000 firms worldwide have ever adopted EDI. Today, most companies have, or will soon implement, some form of ERP system, and it is the need to integrate procurement data—item numbers, descriptions, contracts, prices, invoice details—with those back-end systems that makes broad agreement on industry standards essential.

FROM EDI TO XML

For the past 25 years, Electronic Data Interchange has been the only real method for electronic transmission of business data between buyers and sellers. As we have already seen, however, although many large companies moved to develop EDI connections at least between their major trading partners, the combination of high maintenance overhead, expensive leased lines, and cumbersome protocol translations meant that EDI was too complicated and too expensive for all but the largest buyers and their key suppliers. It has always been prohibitively expensive for small firms—suppliers or buying companies. It is safe to say that any company that can afford to have an EDI link probably already has it. In fact, only 300,000 firms worldwide have adopted

EDI, and even retail industries, where fast-moving goods most merit this sort of electronic exchange of business information, have fewer than 20% of their suppliers connected.

In 1996, however, a potentially revolutionary business data interchange standard came to the market with a new Extensible Markup Language (XML), which promised for the first time to provide a simple and affordable solution for secure exchange of transactional business data between firms.

XML was everything that EDI was not. Because EDI assumed (correctly) that bandwidth would be extortionately expensive, EDI messages use a compressed and confusing set of codes, and much of the explanatory metadata that help programmers to decipher and debug messages has been left out. These compressed message formats not only make EDI transactions expensive and difficult to code, but they are inherent to the code itself, which essentially means it can't be fixed. All of this makes EDI programming difficult and expensive, and EDI programmers often difficult to train and to keep. This is particularly true today, when EDI programmers—with a wary eye on XML—are becoming increasingly concerned about being trapped in an old technology that may become entirely obsolete in a matter of months.

XML is not a language itself, but a *meta-language standard* that provides a flexible and inexpensive way to create common data formats. A subset of the Standard Generalized Markup Language (SGML), XML uses plain text to provide *tags* that describe both the format for the data and the data content itself. These tags can be used to easily identify key pieces of everyday business data—an address, a price, or a customer name—and to code for a transfer of that data to respective symbols in other applications. This means that once XML tags are programmed to recognize and match against another application's symbols, that application can continuously receive transfers of data without having to redefine these links. Therefore, if all suppliers use an agreed-upon XML standard, once the interactive format is defined, the in-house system can read electronic data messages from any supplier using that set of XML data tags.

To make things even more sensible, each XML document is self-defining and carries with it a Document Type Definition (DTD) that provides an explanation of the data language used in the document. In this way, although XML does not affect the way that companies label or organize their current data, it means that any system that supports XML can read and understand the data inside the document.

Creating DTDs is not difficult, and unlike Java and other codes, XML is easily learned and manipulated. But although each company could reformat their current systems to understand various DTDs, a proliferation of various and overlapping DTDs helps no one. For that reason, many hundreds of interested companies, including key IT industry leaders such as Sun Microsystems, IBM, and Microsoft are moving quickly to set industry standards for DTDs that are universally accepted by suppliers and vendors in their industry verticals. For those companies that have significant investments in EDI, there are a number of translators that will, with varying degrees of effectiveness, attempt to transform EDI into an XML format, or to break out the EDI codes into readable XML symbols, using an EDI parser.

In 1998, the Data Interchange Standards Association (DISA) conceded that XML as a Web-based technology would very likely replace the traditional ANSI X12 EDI as the business-to-business standard for business data exchange. For buyers, this means that they suddenly have potential direct electronic access to secure business file data transfer from small or specialist suppliers who would never have been able to participate in a program of EDI. For suppliers, they now have a relatively simple and inexpensive way to communicate directly with buyers.

However, as always, the devil is in the details, and there is still no true agreement on cross-industry standards for protocols at the product labeling or business transaction levels, and many groups within each industry are still struggling to come to terms with different variations. For example, if your company is in the financial services arena, it is likely that your agreed XML standards will be based on those agreed to by the 6,800 member banks of the SWIFT cooperative (Society for Worldwide Interbank Financial Telecommunications). Electronic component suppliers will use XML data formats agreed to by RosettaNet. Insurance firms will use ACORD standard protocols. If as a supplier, you sell horizontal product lines—office supplies or travel services—to companies in a variety of industries, you may need to adhere to standards set by members of the OAGI (Open Applications Group, Inc.). Exchanges built on Ariba's software use the cXML (Commerce XML) protocol, while those using Commerce One are based on xCBL (XML Common Business Library).

XML

Automotive Rentals, Inc. in Mount Laurel, N.J., a global fleet-management company, maintains extensive data on the vehicles under management in multiple systems around the world. But if a customer wanted to see a consolidated report on all of its vehicles worldwide, ARI had a difficult job coming up with the information. The problem resulted from information buried in multiple database systems, stored under different database schemas.

Realizing how difficult it would be to get every unit in the company to agree on a common database system, the company turned to XML, says Bill Kwelty, manager of customer services. The company was able to get everybody to agree to a set of common fields, which it defined in XML as a document type definition file. These fields represent the data customers will likely want.

With agreement on the fields and the distribution of the corresponding set of XML tags, the company, using the Bluestone XML server, is able to generate XML documents in response to customer requests for information. By using XML, the company avoided having to build a data mart or data warehouse and eliminates all the problems associated with updating and synchronizing data marts. "Now everyone has access to the information without our having to build and maintain a data warehouse," Kwelty says. All anybody needs is the ability to parse an XML document.

Source: Alan Radding,"XML: The Language of Integration," *InformationWeek Online,* November 1, 1999, p. 4. Used with permission.

Accordingly, the greatest obstacle remaining is that (as of 2001) there are multiple proposed XML protocol standards under development through major industry collaborations, and although they all profess to have the same goal—to develop well-accepted schema, or vocabularies, that will provide standardized and predictable dictionaries of XML terms, and repositories that will store and help manage the product descriptions—they are not all necessarily working in harmony. These include:

- CommerceNet, a business consortium, which is developing eCO Framework X.

- RosettaNet, a consortium of electronics companies with a supply chain focus, is possibly the most advanced and influential of the several standards groups, and membership includes powerful enterprises such as Federal Express, Cisco, American Express, and EDS. RosettaNet has not only developed XML standards for product catalogs, including a dictionary of 3,600 terms describing things such as components, parts, and finished IT products, but has also devised over 100 XML-based business processes. Its goal is to produce a full supply chain XML standard for the IT industry.

- Vendors such as Ariba and Commerce One also are defining their own XML schema, or industry vocabularies, as they build their online trading communities. Commerce One has created a common business library (CBL) as part of a government grant from the U.S. National Institute for Standards and Technology and has made its DTD repository available through its Web site. Ariba, too, has put a great amount of energy into supporting commerce XML (cXML) and into developing its XML Interoperability Bus Architecture, a framework that will support third-party software integration based on standard XML interfaces.

- The Open Buying Initiative (OBI) is a standard for Internet-based business-to-business purchasing that is sponsored by a group of large buying organizations and their suppliers. Mostly focused on indirect materials, the idea was to provide a mechanism for incorporating EDI within OBI objects, but is in reality fairly limited, and few suppliers have moved to adopt the standard.

- The BizTalk framework, sponsored by Microsoft, helps to convert business objects from other applications into XML and is closely linked to another Microsoft creation, the BizTalk.org Web site that also acts as a repository for XML schema. Members include Boeing, the Open Applications Group, some of the most influential ERP vendors—Baan, PeopleSoft, and SAP—as well as Ariba and Commerce One.

■ The Organization for the Advancement of Structured Information Standards, a nonprofit and vendor-neutral consortium, also has plans for its own repository of XML schema, accessible on a Web site called XML.cor.

■ The Open Applications Group, Inc.—members include Lucent Technologies, Ford, Microsoft, and IBM—is a nonprofit consortium focusing on best practices and process-based XML content for e-business and application integration. It is the largest publisher of XML-based messages for business software interoperability.

Although there are some who lament the end of EDI and still feel more comfortable with the security of the direct and proprietary link between buyers and sellers, few can doubt that XML is the way forward. The greater hesitation, for many companies, is to abandon what for large companies can be multimillion dollar investments in these EDI links. Nonetheless, the writing is on the wall.

Government and E-Procurement

Procurement budgets for local, state, and federal governments, universities, public agencies, and the military account for a significant percentage of all the procurement activity in our economy. Adoption of e-procurement methods by these groups will greatly bolster the uptake of e-procurement among companies in the economy, and will have a strong influence on the development and evolution of e-procurement tools and techniques.

- Government and military purchasing is big business, responsible for sustaining many suppliers worldwide.

- The government has the ability to move its suppliers toward a more sophisticated, online approach to procurement.

- Both private firms and government agencies are now developing trade portals and engaging in pilot programs for providing online purchasing.

I f there is one sector in the economy where e-procurement can and will have an enormous effect, it is government. Consider the procurement costs in the U.S. alone for federal, state, and local governments, for the military, for state universities,

We should be careful not to underestimate the effect that government endorsement and participation of e-procurement can mean to both the industry and to the economy.

junior colleges, school systems, and veterans' hospitals. The figures are staggering. The combined federal and state government procurement costs each year for materials and services purchased from private firms is estimated to be almost $1 trillion. Federal government spending alone on materials and services in 2000 was around $550 billion. If it were possible for the federal government, with its vast economy of scale and massive need for MRO materials, to reduce the cost of procurement only 20% (which, as we have seen, is not uncommon with e-procurement initiatives in the private sector), taxpayers could realize annual savings of $110 billion.[1]

Similarly, the combined European Union (EU) government procurement spending was $778 billion in 2000, and given the even greater level of participation of government—in areas such as public transportation, utilities, national airlines and airports, and their nationally sponsored health care systems—the impact of e-procurement could be even more profound. That is equally true for Japan and nations of the Pacific Rim, where huge investment in national IT and telecommunications infrastructure make e-procurement initiatives a logical next step.[2]

ADVANTAGES WILL NOT BE IN SAVINGS ALONE

Government and military purchasing not only accounts for a huge amount of taxpayer revenue, but it is also big business, responsible for sustaining an enormous number of suppliers throughout the world. And although that sort of buying clout in the hands of a single conglomerate might be worrisome, many would argue that the benevolent focus of government means that—much as spending on IT originally revolved around the needs of the military industrial complex—a strong move toward electronic business by the federal government could serve to dramatically stimulate and upgrade the economy in the coming years.

We should be careful not to underestimate the effect that government endorsement and participation in this area can mean. In the same way (but to a much greater extent) that large purchasing conglomerates, such as Covisint and GlobalNetXchange, can force their supplier base to move toward online purchasing and adhere to certain industry-acceptable standards for communications protocols, so the federal government can move its many hundreds of thousands of suppliers—large and small—toward a more sophisticated, online approach to procurement. In adopting business-to-business e-commerce, the federal government can provide an enormous incentive for suppliers to become Web-enabled and can stimulate economic growth in this area. It can thereby provide an important endorsement for a shift toward the efficiencies and accountability that comes from procuring online, and encourage much broader use of the Internet generally, with all the related developments in software, business startups, and stock market buoyancy that that entails.

Given the advantages of e-procurement, both for government agencies and for the economy as a whole, however, government at all levels in the U.S. has until lately been surprisingly timid in its efforts to move toward online procurement. This is probably in part because of the preoccupation with the Y2K concerns that so dominated much of the last several years. It is probably also due to a combination of the lack of private sector incentives that have been driving e-procurement among businesses, and the same sort of change management problems that tend to plague large, private firms. After all, although as citizens we tend to view the government as a single entity, those involved with government agencies and departments will explain that creating an "enterprise-wide" initiative can be virtually impossible given the overlapping and often competing power interests.

Certainly, however, there is a growing sense of the need for "e-government" to make government services more efficient, more accessible, and easier for the public, and many argue that along with broader e-government initiatives, such as electronic voting, online tax services, and bill payment, e-procurement particularly will be the impetus to move government into the electronic age. It may well be that the original "reengineering the government" effort that was initiated with only limited effect nearly 10 years ago was premature, at least in part because the technology—in the form of the Internet and the growing number of software support platforms—simply wasn't there to allow for a wholesale restructuring.

GOVERNMENT-TO-BUSINESS E-COMMERCE

If there is, however, any one area where the U.S. federal government has begun to take advantage of the power of the Internet for other than general information services, it is in the arena of e-procurement. And for anyone who has ever been involved in the complex and time-consuming process used by governments for tendering and purchasing, improvements on this front will come as a welcome relief. In fact, the Gartner Group predicts that government-to-business e-commerce spending will expand dramatically in the next few years, from its current $1.5 billion to more than $6 billion by 2005.[3]

Much of the credit for this sudden, if limited, appreciation by government of the advantages of online procurement can be attributed to private firms that have been quick to realize the potential for providing online trading portals and exchange services for the myriad number of firms involved in government purchasing. Although still very limited in their functionality, these private/public alliances are the first step toward developing a broader set of government-based e-procurement services.

One good example is PartnershipAmerica.com, a portal site developed and launched by Ingram Micro, Inc. that puts private firms in touch with federal, state, and local government high-technology buyers. VerticalNet recently purchased GovCon.com, a portal that provides suppliers with a number of services, including Bidradar.com, which acts as a search engine and email delivery system for awards and procurement opportunities issued by the federal government. Bidradar.com also allows potential suppliers to register and qualify online, and provides access to sample bids, contracts, and other government forms.

Similarly, Fedmarket.com, designed and administered by Wood River Technologies, provides an e-procurement online portal site that today focuses mostly on information technology and construction purchasing for state and federal government contracts, and includes vendor and buyer directories and ties to government procurement law databases, registration information, a library of forms, and links to federal assistance centers. The site also provides access to several databases that help the potential bidder to search Web pages for opportunities and competitive tenders being issued by the government.

Although most of these efforts still remain at an informational level only, hints of what is surely to come can be seen with ventures such as the agreement between Bank of America and NIC Commerce to form a company that will provide state and local governments with an electronic purchasing and payment service for their private sector suppliers. This is the first step toward providing transactional services online, including search engines and databases of preferred suppliers, online ordering, and reconciliation and payment services.

The federal government itself has sponsored several important initiatives recently that support the underlying structural changes that will be necessary in order to make online procurement effective. Traditionally, one of the biggest problems facing suppliers hoping to bid on government contracts has been simply learning of opportunities well enough in advance to be able to prepare a well-developed response. The Office of Federal Procurement Policy has now put forward plans to provide a single, governmentwide portal accessible on the Internet, which would provide all relevant information on contract announcements and awards.[4] Similarly, the Government Contracting Group now provides—for a subscription fee of $1,000—a real-time online service that displays new RFPs, procurement announcements, and bid notices.[5]

There are also a number of e-procurement programs being initiated at the state level. One promising venture is in Massachusetts, where the state has begun a broad e-procurement program that involves its 154 departments as well as some 350 Massachusetts towns and cities. Using software from Intelisys, a recent pilot program cut transaction costs by as much as 72%, while reducing the delivery cycle from weeks to days.[6]

Admittedly, none of this compares particularly well with the flurry of e-procurement activity that is occurring in the private sector, but it does give a glimpse of future activities. Possibly more important, the magnitude of government procurement has meant that e-procurement software vendors such as Ariba and Commerce

One are now offering services that include government contracting and RFP listings to assist suppliers wishing to sell to the government electronically.

The EU too has struggled with efforts in the e-procurement arena. Burdened with restrictive procurement procedures, layers of processes and approvals, and a much greater number of government-sponsored tenders (public procurement accounts for 11.5% of the EU's GDP), they have additional issues concerning cross-border trade, price differences between countries, and hidden and protected contracting that give them a unique incentive to move toward Internet-based procurement.

In fact, as with Minitel, France's precurser to the Internet, the EU first began tentative moves toward a form of electronic procurement as far back as 1994, when they established a public procurement initiative, the Système d'Information pour les Marchés Publics (Simap), that was based on CD-ROMs and a dial-up database and provided information concerning public tenders, RFPs, purchasing authorities, and bid requirements. In time, they migrated that program to the Internet, introducing search engines for finding vendors, opportunities, contracts, and guidance.

There is little doubt that the Simap system—particularly with a growing number of Internet-based enhancements—is cost effective. While moving the program online has cost an estimated EUR 10 million, cancellation of the massive paper version that has been distributed in the past will account for savings of EUR 70 million each year. Part of the purpose of the program is to reduce the long waiting periods involved in public tendering. The paper-based system meant that purchasing agencies were required to wait for at least 52 days between advertising and awarding a contract. They now estimate that the process could be reduced to between 10 and 15 days by using an online system.

As is still too often the case within the EU, the real issue is participation and compliance, with the majority of public sector contracts still being awarded (in violation of EU rules) without a public posting. Today, despite the growing functionality offered through the Internet system, less than one-third of public sector contracts are actually publicized at all.[7]

The one key area of savings that the EU governments have (and that the U.S. does not, except for Medicare and Medicaid programs, have) that provides an enormous incentive to cut costs and improve service is healthcare. As part of national systems, procurement in the healthcare services is notoriously inefficient. There are more than 11,000 hospitals across the EU, accounting for the equivalent of some $66 billion in supplies each year. Very few of those hospitals have the extra funding or the IT skills to invest in any sort of online e-procurement system.

As in the U.S., early solutions have sprung up from the private sector. Smartmission, already trading in eight European countries, is an Internet e-market for medical supplies—MRO, food, drugs, utilities, and many other items necessary for the running of a hospital—that claims to be able to cut typical purchasing transaction costs for a hospital by 60% to 80%. A second exchange, GloMediX, already available in four European countries, focuses just on medical supplies, but contends they will be able to cut the cost of a typical purchase from EUR 145 to EUR 5. These types of online exchanges provide the same advantages for hospitals as they do for small buyers—collectively, they can place larger orders and negotiate for better discounts.[8]

The government in China, too, has moved into the e-procurement arena, with the announcement of China Trade World.com, a trade portal that will help foreign businesses to import goods to more than 180,000 Chinese manufacturing and production sites.

In order to appreciate the direction in which government e-procurement is moving, however, it is helpful to look at Singapore—the self-proclaimed "knowledge island"—where they have already made great progress toward a government-wide Internet-based e-procurement system. Their broader e-government plan is to provide a single point of contact—a portal known as GeBIZ—that gives all citizens and businesses direct, 24-hour access to a comprehensive and integrated government network. Well ahead of most nations in terms of implementation, the GeBIZ portal will be part of a much more comprehensive system of government information and payment services, through which it will soon be possible to conduct all government-related business—payment of parking fines, utilities, and taxes, for example—online.

Part of that e-government offering is a fast-developing set of e-procurement services that combines many of the elements of both public and private purchasing at a level only now being contemplated by many trend-leading private firms in the rest of the world. The GeBIZ portal will provide not only an informational forum for government-sponsored tenders and RFPs, but also a broad variety of procurement-related services, including allowing suppliers to post their product catalogs online, online auctions, and online invoicing and order tracking. Most importantly, there are plans to provide for direct integration between the payment and financial systems of government agencies and back-office ERP software (PeopleSoft, SAP, Oracle, etc.) of private firms. Although online purchase transactions are currently limited to a maximum of $17,000, once security issues are overcome, it is likely that up to 80% of all government procurement will be conducted through the GeBIZ portal.[9]

Although it is unlikely that either U.S. or EU governments will ever contemplate the level of enforced consensus between government ministries and private organizations that is part of the culture of Singapore, it is fascinating to see how quickly the unique combination of government funding and cultural cohesion have combined to drive e-procurement forward so effectively.

THE MILITARY

Defense procurement is another major area of government spending that has enormous potential for cost savings and improved efficiencies. Many will remember the colossal row that erupted during the mid-1980s concerning inflated prices for the MRO equivalents of military materials—hundreds of dollars paid for a toilet seat or a coffee pot—and although in fact few of these accusations turned out to be accurate (most were eventually explained away as anomalies in the U.S. Department of Defense's accounting methodology), the U.S. military, particularly, has since been seen as the epitome of bad procurement practice.

Despite this unenviable reputation—and the end of the Cold War and the Peace Dividend, which has meant that procurement budgets were slashed dramatically since their heyday in the 1980s—the U.S. and the EU nations, particularly, still have massive defense procurement needs. The good news is that cooperation between the military and Internet-minded private defense contractors is promising to revolutionize the Defense Department's approach to procurement.

This move toward e-procurement is taking several paths. First, major suppliers to the military are moving rapidly toward streamlining their own purchasing through dedicated one-to-many enterprise e-procurement systems. General Electric provides a good example of the e-procurement reforms that are beginning to develop among the military's supplier community. GE Aircraft Engines (GE's aerospace division) is the world's largest manufacturer of aircraft engines. As part of GE's general pledge to quickly move all of its operating units toward e-procurement, Aircraft Engines has begun an online initiative that will provide portal access to over 400 suppliers of spare parts and maintenance materials. The service will include not only online catalogs, but online tendering, order fulfillment, tracking, payment, and access to technical information.

Similarly, Lockheed Martin's missile division is using its SAP system to provide enterprise ORM and MRO desktop purchasing to employees. Employees are now able to browse supplier catalogs electronically and to purchase and track delivery of indirect materials online. Lower production costs due to the efficiencies gained through these types of e-procurement initiatives by contractors promise to be passed on, at least in part, to the military.

A second area of intense e-procurement activity is being sponsored by the U.S. Department of Defense, which began the Joint Electric Commerce Program Office in 1988, using mostly EDI technologies, and has gone a long way toward developing paperless procurement business practices over the past decade. In 1999, the Defense Department announced a strategy that will encourage electronic procurement throughout the military, and although it still requires greater flexibility and functionality in terms of online payment and order fulfillment, it already claims to complete nearly 80% of procurement electronically.

But the area of the most frenetic activity in terms of defense-related online procurement comes with the recent and rapid development of industry-wide e-markets that provide an online trading community that is independent of any one company or large contractor. As with other e-markets, these trading communities have been sponsored, for the most part, by consortiums of interested and interrelated organizations.

One of the first major initiatives in this area was Exostar, an e-market founded by Boeing, Lockheed Martin, Raytheon, and BAE Systems that focuses on indirect materials purchasing for these large contractors. The amount of materials procured through this online exchange is expected to be over $70 billion, which would account for just less than one-fifth of all defense sector procurement spending. As with most vertical exchanges, several other competing trading portals have arisen to challenge Exostar. These include MyAircraft (founded by Honeywell and United Technologies), AviationX, Tradeair, and Aerospan.

There are many more examples, and each week brings new announcements—by state and federal departments, universities, and national health systems—of intentions to participate in auctions or to sponsor or participate in e-markets—all anxious to take advantage of online procurement opportunities. *The sheer magnitude of total government spending—in the U.S. and in the rest of the world—provides a market opportunity so enticing that software vendors, private e-markets, and auction sites, are already scrambling to incorporate the security, contract, and tendering functionality that is required for government bidding.* It is not a market that any vendor would choose to ignore, and once ignited, may prove to be a powerful incentive to private companies, to the e-procurement industry at large, and to the global economy as a whole.

ENDNOTES

1. "Business-to-Government E-Commerce Procurement: Online Centers, Databases, and Tools," *SolutionCentral Daily Briefing,* September 1, 2000, p. 1; "The Next Revolution," *The Economist,* www.economist.com, June 24, 2000, p. 3.

2. "The Next Revolution," *The Economist,* www.economist.com, June 24, 2000, p. 3.

3. "Banking Giant Forms Government E-Procurement Company," *E-Commerce Times,* part of NewsFactor Network (www.NewsFactor.com), July 7, 2000, p. 2.

4. For a full account of e-government projects, see the FCW Web page at www.fcw.com.

5. "Business-to-Government E-Commerce Procurement: Online Centers, Databases, and Tools," *SolutionCentral Daily Briefing,* September 1, 2000, pp. 6–7.

6. "E-Procurement: Unleashing Corporate Purchasing Power," ©2001 Time Inc., all rights reserved, www.fortune.com/sections/eprocurement2000.

7. Houlder, Vanessa, "Trading Towards a Common Market," in "Understanding E-Procurement," *The Financial Times,* Winter 2000, pp. 24–25.

8. "A Spoonful of Sugar," *The Economist,* www.economist.com, July 1, 2000, pp. 1–2.

9. "Island Site," *The Economist,* www.economist.com, June 24, 2000, p. 2.

9 The Future of E-Procurement

Objective

Understanding the eight key trends in the evolution of e-procurement can help when devising a company strategy.

- Development of XML as a standard will greatly improve intersystems connectivity.
- Industry growth will continue with both corporate and network-based e-procurement solutions.
- There will remain two different purchasing paths, although the line between them will continue to blur.
- Consolidation of vertical e-marketplaces.
- Pressure from customers to provide all-inclusive solutions.
- Value of strategic sourcing will come in question for spot markets and commodity buying over the Internet.
- Roles of procurement specialists will change greatly.
- Government spending e-procurement will increase and influence the uptake of online purchasing solutions among private firms.

There can be no
doubt, given the
potential cost savings and
market expansion that e-
procurement can bring to
both buyers and sellers,
that most companies are ready to begin developing an e-
procurement strategy.

But given the volatility and complexity of this fast-evolving marketplace, how can a company know which approach to take?

But given the volatility and complexity of this fast-evolving marketplace, how can a company know which approach to take? Will enterprise applications become completely obsolete, giving way to third-party providers? Will the benefits of low negotiated price and near-instantaneous buying mean that most indirect, and even direct, materials will soon be purchased through e-markets?

There are several things upon which most market analysts would agree.

STANDARDS

The development of XML as a standard, different though it may still be for various industries, will provide the basis for a completely different and greatly improved level of intersystems connectivity. From now on, XML and future derivations of it will mean that even small suppliers can easily transfer their catalogs, contract terms, and invoices to any buyer directly, cheaply, and securely via the Internet. This will, in many ways, revolutionize the nature of business information transfer. There is little doubt that these standards will eventually fall into place, so what effect will this interoperability have on the e-procurement marketplace?

ENTERPRISE VERSUS E-MARKET MODELS

It is probably safe to bet that, at least in the next five years, neither secure one-to-many enterprise solutions nor third-party sponsored electronic trading communities will completely disappear, nor will they completely dominate the e-procurement marketplace. Although the early successes of the e-marketplace made many enthusiasts predict a complete shutdown of the enterprise-owned, one-to-many model, it seems unlikely that this will happen. To the contrary, fears concerning reliability, security, and overcoming cultural hesitancy to sever trusted trading relationships with individual suppliers have meant that in the U.S.—and to an even greater extent in Europe—senior management has been hesitant to move toward a strategy where there is exclusive dependence on outsourcing firms or on hosted trading communities for purchasing direct, or even mission-critical, MRO materials.

But, equally powerful arguments can be made in favor of the continued growth and popularity of the e-market trading hubs, particularly as auction-type exchanges drive down prices, and market creators and ASPs move to provide a more value-added service. What is more likely is that there will remain two essentially different types of offerings—the buyer-sponsored enterprise model and the third-party-sponsored exchange model—and that each of these two areas will see dramatic changes in terms of focus and consolidation in the coming months.

DIRECT VERSUS INDIRECT

It is likely that the purchase of indirect and direct goods will continue to require different approaches, with an emphasis on spot markets and impersonal supplier-buyer relationships becoming the rule for indirect and, to a lesser extent, less complex MRO materials. Although the separate paths traditionally reserved for indirect and direct materials are blurring in some ways, the fact is that some materials (indirect) lend themselves better to exchanges and catalogs, while others, (MRO parts and mission-critical direct materials) have very different characteristics and may need a completely dedicated set of processes, tools, and vendors. Bulk direct materials may profit from spot-market type buying, but many complex or highly specialized manufactured components will still require a more personal buyer-seller relationship, even if that process is electronically enhanced.

CONSOLIDATION OF E-MARKET VERTICALS

As we have seen, consolidation within the third-party electronic trading community verticals has already begun. Many buying companies will want to outsource large pieces of their procurement work, and suppliers, often from other nations and with limited IT abilities outside of a capacity to log onto the Internet, will be anxious to use these online markets to sell their goods. But in order to be effective and to differentiate themselves in an extraordinarily competitive marketplace, these electronic trading communities themselves will face increasing demands to provide buyers and sellers with a full set of procurement services that essentially underwrite, or guarantee, the success of the transaction.

But, as we have also seen, this is no easy task. The value of these trading hubs comes from their ability to engage, in some cases, thousands of suppliers and buyers from around the world. Yet, each of these trading partners will have a requirement for integrating transaction information into their respective ERP systems. At its most basic, that means that the ASP or exchange host will need to ensure that the transaction between buyer and seller actually takes place, and that means that order fulfillment, tracking, payment, and delivery services will need to be provided electronically. If these third parties are to ever move successfully into a direct materials market, they will also need to provide a much more complex group of services associated with automated inventory replenishment and logistics services, or at least be able to communicate digitally and act as an interface between the supply chain and ERP systems of the sellers and the buyers. In order to support international sales, this also means supporting different systems for tax, export, language, and currency.

Although many exchange sites abrogate these responsibilities, claiming that they serve only as an open portal for negotiation and sales, these more limited auction-type portals will almost certainly remain limited to sales of non-mission-critical indirect materials. Moreover, in each vertical market, the unceasing drive among the many auction sites to differentiate themselves will mean that only those that provide the most full-function and reliable service will survive. The inevitable evolution of these sites is toward fuller functionality or extinction.

In short, those that survive will need to offer supply chain management expertise as opposed to simple purchasing leverage. These e-markets are increasingly likely—through a combination of partnerships, mergers, acquisitions, and XML interoperability standards—to take on much of the responsibility for leading practices, insurance, legal, tie-in to payment systems, and even logistics and CRM (see Figure

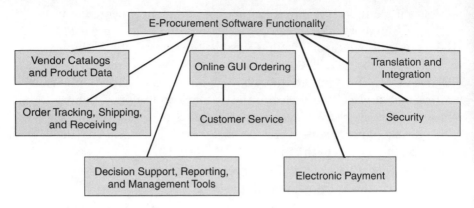

Figure 9.1 E-procurement software functionality.

9.1). If any of these areas are overlooked, it breaks down the continuity of the supply chain. As mentioned earlier, most estimates these days set the probable number of survivors for each vertical market at no more than three or four.

Moreover, the influential and financially powerful market creators that are driving many of these new trading communities are certainly not going to be content with providing e-procurement services alone. Although their initial focus was to provide an attractive forum where large companies could contact sellers in order to save money and sellers could expand their markets by contacting multiple buyers, the strategic aim of these market creators has to be to dominate and diversify—to create new revenue streams through the deeper relationships that this type of commerce community will afford to them. Much like the Sabre Reservation system for American Airlines, which still provides the company more revenue than their air services, these giant-sponsored trading communities will not be content to provide online auctions alone, in the future.

SINGLE-SOLUTION SUPPLIERS

Just as the pressures to move toward integrated solutions are forcing a consolidation in the vertical e-market trading communities, it is also very likely that there will be a move toward consolidation—to probably three to four major solution providers—for internal, enterprise e-procurement solutions. Although the enterprise-based software platforms and the one-to-many model may be the solution of choice for direct goods, companies will also like access to e-markets for ORM, some MRO materials, and bulk-buy direct goods. Customers will not want to have two separate systems, even if tl approaches to buying vary greatly. These two paths will m customers seek a single system for all purchasing-related a(that will provide access to e-markets and provide a stable pl. for maintaining more traditional one-to-one relationships witl cialist vendors. In short, direct and indirect will remain differe approach, but will become the same in terms of systems delivery

Fearing encroachment on their early domination of direct procurement, and realizing that companies like Ariba and Commerce One are finding success in Internet-based procurement of indirect goods, the leading ERP vendors—SAP, PeopleSoft, Baan, Oracle— have all added integrated Web-based procurement modules to their manufacturing suites. These ERP vendors have long been involved with attempts to automate the procurement process of direct materials for manufacturing firms, and they see the capacity for Web-based procurement as a natural extension of their core competency (see Chapter 5).

In fact, beyond just the integration of direct and indirect procurement approaches, the market is crying out for a platform scenario that provides all the many pieces for buying and selling digitally—a system for both indirect and direct materials, with both enterprise and external e-market focus, that automates the entire purchasing chain, and provides a seamless link between order fulfillment, payment, delivery, and ultimately inventory replenishment. And most companies don't want to spend millions of dollars and hundreds of years of man-hours implementing and integrating disparate systems. There are usually at least 5 potential software platforms that any company can turn to for e-procurement, and often more than 20. All of this creates a significant integration challenge, and although Enterprise Application Integration (EAI) solutions and XML will continue to make inter-system integration more efficient—both inside and outside the company firewall—the advantages of a fully-integrated solution (as opposed to one cobbled together) will continue to be pressed strongly by buyers.

The problem is that, at present, no vendor is able to provide that level of service. The different histories and natures of ERP, procurement, and supply chain systems mean that, though with some effort they may provide interoperability, it is unlikely in the near term that one company could provide all of the needed functionality on a single platform. Part of the problem is simply that companies themselves seldom have a single, seamless platform internally, having itched together, by necessity, ERP, CRM, e-commerce, supply chain, and e-procurement solutions from different vendors.

As a result, many vendors have been scrambling to expand their offerings through a combination of internal software development and alliances and mergers with related vendors.

One good example is the partnership between Ariba, supply-chain management software vendor i2 Technologies, and IBM, an arrangement announced in early 2000. Ariba's combined procurement platform of both enterprise and e-market services will use IBM's WebSphere Internet commerce software to integrate procurement with i2's TradeMatrix supply chain software, using Web-Method's server to direct data between the different platforms. This arrangement, they assert, "creates a full, integrated package that ranges from transactions to logistics and payment handling."

But there are also an entirely new group of more adventurous, all-inclusive third-party providers. These organizations—companies like INC2inc, Ventro and VerticalNet—are assembling their own end-to-end suites from various vendors, and may become the proprietors of large and powerful independent infrastructure platforms. Most have their origins in vertical industries and, appreciating the fact that much of what they do in terms of providing a procurement platform can easily be transferred to other horizontal and vertical buying and selling groups, they are now able to license use of these integrated platforms to others. VerticalNet, for example, which began as an informational portal for more than 40 sectors, has acquired exchange software-maker Tradeum and catalog aggregation maker Isadora to create an e-marketplace architecture for nearly 60 portals, and is hoping to license the package to other customers. Similarly, Ventro, which creates and runs vertical e-marketplaces in diverse areas ranging from healthcare (Broadlane) to plumbing (Industria) and the ill-fated Chemdex (scientific commodities), provides a full ASP outsourcing service for suppliers and buyers that uses its XML-based middleware product suite (MarketLink) to integrate vertical marketplaces with a company's e-procurement system.

But even these types of unified platforms may have their drawbacks. Critics are quick to explain that "one-stop shopping" is not necessarily the best answer for every company. Not every alliance results in the best-of-breed products that a company may want to purchase, and too often these types of alliances leave an uneven level of functionality among the different parts, with no recourse to choosing alternative vendors. These groups suffer from accusations that such a "take it or leave it" approach may inhibit a company's flexibility in the future. Many firms with the capacity to buy and implement systems in-house prefer to be able to tune systems according to their strengths.

VENDOR RATIONALIZATION

All of this means that the value and need for strategic sourcing has come under fire. The tendency for trading hubs and the e-marketplace is to move to many suppliers instead of to just a few. At issue is the fact that the whole value of vendor rationalization and strategic sourcing comes from consolidation and leverage of a company's best and most trusted suppliers. The basis for successful strategic sourcing is therefore to restrict the number of preferred vendors, and yet with the expansion of e-market portals, the trend is moving in the opposite direction. The logic behind the Internet-based auction is to treat all materials as commodities, driving prices down. That means, generally, the more vendors, the fiercer the competition, and the higher the likelihood of a lower price for the buyer. In this new world, vendors are no longer true partners at all.

Most analysts believe that in this type of buying environment, suppliers will increasingly need to show buying companies that there is merit to a close and personal relationship, and that buyers should forgo the low-price auction approach in favor of a service that is more reliable, or that has other distinct advantages. But in tandem with the competitive forces of consolidation that are already starting to trim down the number of vertical trading hubs, many analysts suggest that, in fact, indirect e-procurement through these e-markets may follow the same path as the EDI networks did for direct goods over the past 20 years, with the number of vendors decreasing rather than increasing, as trading hubs move to clarify their product offerings and provide distinctive, value added services. After all, it is in the sellers' best interest to avoid the low-cost race to the bottom.

THE CHANGING ROLE OF PROCUREMENT SPECIALISTS

Probably all of this will be reflected in a changing nature of the role of procurement specialists. For one thing, systems—ERP, supply chain management APS systems, and in-house e-procurement systems—will soon eliminate manual paper, fax, and phone-based activities, freeing up many procurement employees. Depending on size, of course, for companies not involved in direct materials procurement, as the entire process becomes automated, the purchasing department may disappear entirely except for a couple of specialist super users who deal with systems issues and exceptions. For manufacturing and distribution companies that deal in direct goods, it is more likely that purchasing agents will truly become business negotiators and specialists, looking for bundled service offerings or other differentiating factors among their suppliers that demonstrate true added value.

GOVERNMENT DRIVEN

Finally, although the massive military and government procurement markets are lagging behind private industry in moving into e-procurement, the combination of public demands for lower cost of government, early moves into collaborative online trading communities and e-markets by private contractors, and the belief that government can help set standards and move the economy toward the more efficient practices of online procurement means that this area will soon see significant growth.

Assessing the Pros and Cons of E-Procurement

Objective

Although there are many strong arguments in favor of adopting an e-procurement strategy, a successful enterprise-wide initiative is not without its challenges:

- For buyers, e-procurement can mean lower transaction costs, faster ordering, a greater choice of suppliers, and less maverick buying.

- For sellers, e-procurement can help to expand sales, reduce operating costs, and improve performance.

- But there are significant difficulties to be addressed in e-procurement projects, including system-to-system integration issues, cost concerns, security issues, new buyer-seller relationships, and a multitude of change management issues.

Whatever the difficulties in developing a strategy, in predicting marketplace changes, and in dealing with significant levels of internal change, when it comes to implementing e-procurement initiatives there are still some notable successes. But most organizations have only just begun to examine their e-business strategies, and have a long struggle ahead. So what are the pros and cons of the situation?

It is estimated that nearly 75% of e-business company initiatives (these include e-commerce projects) will fail within the next two years.

THE PROS

For Buyers

The pros of e-procurement for buying organizations have already been discussed, but these are worth looking at again. For ORM and the majority of MRO, whether an enterprise solution or a subscription to an ASP or a trading portal, all purchasing can be done by employees from the desktop, saving hours of comparison browsing and misordering. This approach frees up purchasing specialists for work on strategic sourcing, and also provides an easy and effective alternative for maverick buying. Overall, these desktop requisition systems for indirect goods save time, and through reduced labor costs, on-contract buying, and best-price purchasing, also save money.

E-market exchanges and auctions—again, particularly within the context of high-volume, low item-cost indirect goods—enable companies to quickly and efficiently participate in real-time bidding in a negotiated commerce environment while realizing cost efficiencies through reduced purchasing costs, access to dynamic market pricing, reduced sourcing cycle time, lower cost of sales, greater access to new geographic markets. In summary, these e-procurement systems promise

- lower transaction costs
- faster ordering
- greater choice of suppliers
- increased efficiency of standardized purchasing processes
- less maverick buying
- the ability for buyers to use their intranet to search for and purchase contract-based and "spot" items from a vast supplier community
- elimination of much of the inefficient paperwork and unnecessary, repetitive steps involved in procuring complex equipment and services
- improvement and streamlining of the workflow of operators and vendors through features such as online project management and knowledge management

For Sellers

Internet-based e-procurement has even more benefits for suppliers, because it seldom requires a large investment in order to participate, and particularly with the industry-focused portals, it allows them to expand their markets, eliminate restrictive, vertical market focus, and many would contend, to compete on merit (that is to say, price and not relationships). For the majority of suppliers, the advantages include:

- *Expanding sales.* By providing electronic catalogs online, directly to the employees and buyers enterprise-wide, or via the e-hubs and electronic trading communities, suppliers are able to greatly expand their sales volumes. This should help reduce sales process costs by nearly 25%. Moreover, suppliers can redefine the focus of their sales forces toward a more consultative sale, and W.W. Grainger estimates vendors could see incremental sales gains of 10% to 20% by selling online.[1]

- *Reducing operating costs.* Once a supplier's systems are able to transfer and receive business data directly to and from the buyers, the supplier can create orders much more quickly and minimize the time and cost of transcription errors so common with paper-based processes.

■ *Improving performance.* Linking to a customer directly and collaborating to ensure accurate and on-time delivery provides better service and lower overall procurement costs to the customer, and can result in much more collaborative buyer-seller relationships. As a preferred supplier, or if the buyer begins to provide forecasts of requirements to its vendors, the supplier can begin to predict and prepare for individual buyer requirements well ahead of time.

THE CONS

As with all revolutionary ideas, implementing a successful e-procurement initiative is dependent upon overcoming several key strategic and tactical obstacles. So far, most companies are not finding it easy. In fact, it is estimated that nearly 75% of e-business company initiatives (these include e-commerce projects) will fail within the next two years. Curiously, this is not for reasons that we might suspect—not because the tools and standards are not yet stable, nor even because the marketplace is unpredictable and volatile. The real problem is that, at least for direct materials, companies too often fail to overcome issues surrounding

■ System-to-system integration, both inside and outside the company firewalls

■ Initial investment costs

■ Security, trust, and supplier-buyer relationships

■ Fundamental changes to procurement business processes and company culture

Let's look at each of these issues.

System-to-System Integration Issues

As we have seen, despite the current level of market hyperbole and the genuine potential of e-procurement when well integrated, the fact is only a handful of large and progressive companies have been able to fully integrate their electronic procurement processes and systems. Most companies, anticipating the cost and effort of integrating or replacing legacy systems, and alarmed by the constantly changing nature of the e-procurement marketplace, have done little to move forward. Of those that have, few have achieved a satisfactory level of systems integration. A recent survey reflects the frustration of procurement specialists:

- Some 40% of the 212 respondents, users of both enterprise resource planning and dedicated electronic purchasing systems, complained they had to use more than one system to do basic purchasing and contracting.

- Another 86% said they wanted a single-entry search engine for doing comparison shopping, but only 25% have this today.

- A third of the purchasing managers said they could not easily place orders against a master contract, even though 94% said they wanted to do so.[2]

The problems involved with systems integration, as anyone who has worked on IT projects can attest, are manifold. How quickly or easily these systems can be integrated is very much dependent, of course, on the level of interoperability and compatibility. Saroja Girishankar put it well: "Fundamental differences range from server platform and programming language to object structures used to create applications to the user interface—either a browser or proprietary piece of software.... If one software suite is written in Java using Enterprise JavaBeans and runs on a UNIX operating system, and the other suite runs on Windows NT, is written in C++, and uses Active Server pages and the Distributed COM model, integration could be a lengthy process."[3]

The low level of technical sophistication among many suppliers is only one issue, compounded by the general lack of systems compatibility within the buyer's own organization. This has tended to undermine the ROI for any e-procurement investment, in that a persistent belief continues among procurement specialists that even if the buying process itself can be enhanced by online e-markets or a closer one-to-many model, the huge variance in supplier systems and present poor levels of reliability means that, particularly for mission-critical direct materials purchasing, the traditional telephone and paper-based invoicing and settlement process would have to continue anyway, if only in parallel or as a backup.

The problems are not made easier by the volatility of the marketplace. Broadly, buyers have two choices. The first is to wait until their ERP vendor makes their system more capable of supporting e-procurement over the Internet (which many are doing). However, critics cite concern that ERP companies don't really have the expertise to develop full-function e-procurement systems based on the latest Web technology, and point to what the market has generally perceived to be a slow start, if not a failure, on the parts of many ERP companies to rise to the challenge of integrating supply chain and APS systems into their traditional accounting and materials management functionality.

A second option for buying companies is to put their money behind one of the major e-procurement suites—such as Ariba or Commerce One—which have quickly moved to provide both enterprise systems and e-market trading functionality. The hope is that a combination of collaborative alliance activity and third-party XML-based integration offerings will provide the level of interoperability with in-house ERP systems that is needed to justify the cost and to provide a fully integrated and reliable solution.

Initial Investment Costs

Although few industry analysts would disagree that the benefits, at least in principle, far outweigh the costs, an e-procurement initiative of any type comes only with significant up-front investment. Obviously, the price of e-procurement applications varies considerably. According to Gartner Group, Trilogy Software costs about $10,000 but Remedy and SupplyWorks average more around $100,000. At the higher end, CommerceOne's MarketSite ranges from $500,000 to $2 million, and Ariba's systems can range from $1 million to several million dollars.[4] As a rule of thumb, an enterprise with an annual revenue of at least $1 billion will typically spend $3 to $4 million to implement e-procurement software, including the systems integration with back-end ERP systems.[5]

However, buying and installing the e-procurement application represents a small fraction of the total expense of implementing e-procurement. Like most enterprise-wide IT implementations, typically less visible costs exceed software purchase fees by 5 or 10 times. These include

- Catalog and content development
- Consulting fees (system implementation, EAI, process improvement, change management)
- Supplier negotiations and assistance
- Education and training
- Licensing, maintenance, and other system-related fees
- System integration
- Non-production hours spent on the project by in-house resources

Appreciating the hesitancy of some companies to come up with this initial investment, many software providers, including Clarus and Usinternetworking, offer a "zero capital" model in which companies essentially rent a system, with very little cost up front, but with monthly subscription fees covering all hardware, software, and support costs.[6]

It is possible, of course, to escape some of these costs, though not all of them, simply by subscribing for e-procurement services through ASPs. There are obvious limitations to an exclusively e-market-based service, but typically, the e-markets and trading hub fees run between 1% and 15% of the value of the transaction, depending on volumes and the types of product being bought and sold. But although Internet portal-based trading hubs and e-marketplaces charge only a subscription, a strong ROI is still almost guaranteed. As previously mentioned, even with these commissions, buyers typically end up saving 10% to 40% on their transactions. With the high level of competition for buyers these days, there will almost certainly be a continuous "race to the bottom" by trading hub sponsors, who will attempt to gain customers by dropping their transaction costs as low as possible. Unfortunately, that type of competitive pressure can bring bad consequences for buyers, as well as good ones, since in order to create profit as competition increases, dotcoms will move to other, less helpful schemes. In fact, as desktop requisitioning has become more widespread, many sell-side Web sites have sought to seduce employees who have recently been given new levels of "empowerment" in purchasing to buy off-contract with them, negotiating one-off discounts, and taking advantage of the very system that was supposed to eliminate this type of maverick buying.

Security, Trust, and Supplier-Buyer Relationships

All of which brings us back to the issue of security, trust, and how to manage the supplier-buyer relationship in this new world of e-procurement.

Security and Encryption Issues One of the issues most often cited by procurement specialists as a significant concern in shifting to an Internet-based form of procurement is that of security. There are two broad areas of concern. First, the Internet itself is, by its nature, inherently insecure. Second, to be effective, an e-procurement initiative requires the exchange of often mission-critical (and therefore very revealing) data between buyers and sellers. For most organizations, procurement-related data—financial data, pricing models, strategic plans, expected new product announcements—can easily be used by competitors to understand company positioning and strategy. Again, there are two key issues to address. First, what information is to be shared? Second, with which partners in the supply chain should it be shared?

In many ways, technology is not the issue, however, because there are (or soon will be) any number of reliable techniques for maintaining the secrecy of data online. Solutions to technical security issues are already coming onto the market. In this regard, Digital Certificate Technology is becoming pivotal to the success of e-procurement, because it promises to provide reliable and verifiable identification of online partners. At the heart of the technology is a *digital signature,* which is based on public key cryptography and makes the electronic transaction legally admissible. Much like an ATM card, which has both a public code and a private PIN, digital signatures identify parties through an independent third-party verification group, and the transaction is electronically validated so that it cannot later be denied. This "undeniability," or "nonrepudiation," becomes critical to procurement transactions.

Another good example of fast evolving security solutions is Public Key Infrastructure (PKI) technology, which is being widely adopted by the U.S. federal government for use on commercial online purchasing and smart card transactions. The program, known as ACES (Access Certificates for Electronic Services), issues digital certificates in real time and online, so that parties conducting business with the government can be identified while engaged on the Internet. Sponsored by a 29-company consortium, these electronic certificates provide government procurement officers with a means of authenticating the identity of the other parties before they begin confidential discussions. These digital certificates will form the basis of real-time, all-electronic government procurement, where no other signature or authorization is required.

In fact, the government is spearheading many of these efforts. They have another program that is similarly based on digital certificates, but also combines the use of *smart cards*—much like standard procurement cards, in that they contain a powerful computer chip embedded in the card so that they can store critical data that ranges from identification codes to transaction data. This combined technology is already being used by the Department of the Treasury and the Department of Defense when exchanging goods internally—often on contracts that are valued at many millions of dollars. And apart from using smart cards and PKI technology themselves, many state governments are already debating legislation that will make these types of "electronic signatures" legally binding. It is only a matter of time before other technologies—fingerprint or retina scan techniques—become the norm.

Still, as a recent survey of European procurement specialists reveals, a hesitancy to complete sensitive procurement transactions online is more often a question of cultural mindset than of practical encryption techniques. In fact, in a PriceWaterhouseCoopers survey of 400 senior business leaders in the UK, Germany, France, and the Netherlands, trust and security issues were named as the two most important factors that were holding back e-procurement progress. It proves how old habits die hard. Nearly two-thirds of respondents said that they sought a "trusted relationship" with vendors before they began to deal with them electronically, and nearly as many—60%—preferred dealing with bricks-and-mortar companies over Internet-only suppliers.

Oddly, though, very few of the companies, even those more advanced in the use of e-procurement, had implemented the security systems available to ensure security. The same report concluded that almost two-thirds of companies relied only on standard password protection when dealing with suppliers over the Internet.[7]

And, of course, security concerns are not limited to the buying company alone. Transparency of data on inventories, price, and performance means that suppliers too are feeling exposed. This type of honesty and transparency may well undermine a supplier's ability to maneuver, as buyers quickly learn to calculate a vendor's costs, profit margins, and stock (and therefore, desperation) levels.

In many ways, though, procurement specialists are talking more about trust issues than technical security. With more and more information being shared between buyers and sellers, a new level of trust becomes necessary—one that pointedly may not exist within the sterile online e-markets, auctions, and exchanges. ORM is one thing, but reliability is everything in purchasing direct materials. Issues of dependability, liability, and security are uppermost in the minds of those procuring direct materials.

All of this again highlights the need, particularly with the procurement of direct goods, for closer buyer-seller relationships than those found through e-markets or online exchanges. Today, suppliers not only need to be dependable, with reasonable price offerings, but in order to participate in the new world of e-procurement, they increasingly are being expected to have the ability to integrate their technical infrastructures closely with the buyer's technical infrastructure and to be able to change their business processes to adhere to the buyer's wish for end-to-end automation. They are also expected to absorb a good deal of the liability, through service level agreements. In the near future, companies will need to move more and more toward collaborative product design and sharing long-term forecasting with their most trusted suppliers.

Again, all of this leads to a conclusion that, in the short term at least, it may well be that the electronic auctions and third-party hubs (trading communities) will concentrate on indirect provision, and the traditional suppliers, made electronically capable, will become the new electronic supplier network for direct inventory.

Fundamental Changes to Procurement Business Processes and Company Culture

Of course, an e-procurement initiative is much more than just a system; it is an entirely new way of working and requires dramatic changes to business processes and to ways of thinking and behaving. In fact, consider for a moment the changes that occur when your company moves from a manual to an electronic procurement environment. These changes include the shift to standardized purchasing contracts and methods, and more strenuous, IT-based authorizations for purchases. Adoption of an e-procurement system also means insisting on the use of that IT system over more familiar fax and phone ordering. There will be greater audit visibility on spending. And, possibly most importantly, the shift from a manual to an electronic purchasing environment will mean changes to roles and responsibilities, with the elimination of many administrative duties, and therefore jobs. Retraining will be necessary so that you are able to take advantage of strategic sourcing opportunities and to redeploy those whose jobs have been eliminated.

Imagine the difficulty of explaining to a company buyer in another state—or possibly even another country—that he or she can no longer use their trusted local supplier because the firm has selected a nationwide vendor instead. And there will be other issues. Information Systems (IS) groups will want to be assured that even when employees are allowed to make PC purchases under preapproved technical parameters, IS will still be notified in advance in order to be prepared to provide setup and help desk support.

Accordingly, there are two key areas of concern that fall under the general heading of change management. The first is initiative-related change management, which is necessary in order to make certain that the project itself is successfully completed. This type of change management requires not only strong project management, but also techniques including

- Assuring that key executives understand the likely risks and benefits of the project before it is begun

- Ensuring enterprise-wide sponsorship among key organizational leaders

- Developing a strong and honest communication plan concerning project approach, schedules, and the likely effect that the end result will have on positions and organizational structure

- Soliciting broad input and participation from different levels of the organization

Aside from the myriad issues that need to be dealt with in order to ensure project success, a second focus of broader change management is necessary. This long-term, company-wide, program of change management is necessary to ensure that corporate-wide purchasing policies are put in place and are incorporated in new working habits, and also to avoid a backlash or an outbreak of maverick buying in the future. Unless these changes to business processes and employee work behavior are specifically dealt with, putting in an automated system may simply allow for old mistakes to be made real-time.

WHY E-PROCUREMENT INITIATIVES FAIL

Hard-learned lessons over the past two years have taught companies that there are many reasons why e-procurement initiatives ultimately fail.

Long-term, company-wide change management is broader in its focus than project success and involves many of the long-term issues that, in the end, result in a successful business transformation. These include rethinking business processes, changing reporting structures, retraining and relocating procurement staff, and altering reward and incentive programs. It also means rethinking and renegotiating relationships with external partners—suppliers or buyers. In this regard, it is important to be realistic about what areas of procurement can be "reengineered," at what time, in what order, and in what timeframe.

"The notion that a company can transform itself into an e-business by simply using a piece of software and adding it to its existing infrastructure is wrong and dangerous," explains Jim Shepherd of AMR Research in a recent report. "Companies must instead incorporate e-business concepts into their overall business strategies. Issues to be aware of include the extension of the enterprise to trading partners, the transformation of relationships with customers and suppliers, radical changes in the order fulfillment process, and the addition or replacement of entire sales channels. These are not decisions for a Web Master or even a CIO alone."[8]

Much of the success of this type of project, then, depends on developing a sound, enterprise-wide e-procurement strategy. Let's now turn to how to develop that strategy, create a program of business change, and successfully implement an e-procurement initiative.

ENDNOTES

1. Brack, Ken, "E-Procurement: The Next Frontier," *Industrial Distribution,* January 1, 2000, p. 2.
2. Booker, Ellis, "Enterprise Users Poke Holes in E-Procurement," *Internetweek Online,* June 4, 1999, pp. 1–2.
3. Girishankar, Saroja, "Making It All Work," *InformationWeek,* Solution Series, June 12, 2000, p. 6. Used with permission.
4. Wilder, Clinton, "Online Procurement Takes Off," *InformationWeek Online,* September 13, 1999, p. 3.
5. Reilly, B., "E-Procurement: A Blueprint for Revolution or Hype?," *Gartner Advisory, Strategic Analysis Report,* The Gartner Group, February 9, 2000.
6. Clarus Company Press Release, November 1, 1999.
7. Ward, Hazel, "Bosses Voice E-Procurement Fears," *Computer Weekly,* July 20, 2000, p. 2.
8. Shepherd, Jim, "E-Business: You Can't Just Add It On or Plug It In," *AMR Research Executive Views,* www.amrresearch.com, November 1, 1999, p. 1.

11 Guiding Principles for Developing an E-Procurement Initiative

Objective

We have learned a lot over the past decade about the best way to implement enterprise-wide initiatives in order to achieve real business results. Accordingly, there are some key guiding principles to consider when approaching an e-procurement initiative:

- An e-procurement initiative, done well, requires dramatic changes in strategy, organization, process and systems.

- There is, as there was with ERP initiatives, a tendency to see an e-procurement project as tactical and technical, and not as strategic.

- It is important that you get early executive involvement and endorsement, that you build a strong case for action, and that you involve all key stakeholders, both within your organization and from the ranks of your suppliers and partners.

As we have seen, an e-procurement initiative, done well, requires dramatic changes in strategy, organization, process, and systems, and affects functions throughout the organization. Although ORM projects tend to be more straightforward, projects focused on the direct materials side—which involves rethinking the entire order fulfillment process, from customer to supplier—require significant changes to the way employees work and how a company organizes its supply chain and purchasing processes.

We have learned a lot about what to do and what not to do to make those enterprise-wide projects a success. The bad news is, implementing companies and consultancies have seldom incorporated this leading-practice project approach, and many, if not most, organizations had a pretty rough time of ERP implementation because they failed to do so.

The U.K. government is a good example. In 1999, U.K. officials had set for themselves a target of cutting some £1 billion from all government procurement costs over the next three years. Having announced their intentions last year of participating in a shopping–mall type of arrangement for ORM materials, which required the use of pretendered catalogs, they have now put a halt to the program, citing fears that the combination of poor back-end systems integration, a volatile marketplace, and the need for rethinking their current paper-based processes means that they are in no position to move forward with an e-procurement program of this scale. For many organizations, this combination of market volatility and a growing appreciation for the need to restructure their processes before implementing sophisticated systems has left them unwilling to commit to a broad e-procurement program.

The good news in all of this is that e-procurement projects can be treated in much the same manner in terms of strategy, project approach, and change management as the enterprise-wide ERP initiatives of the last five years. We have learned a lot about what to do and what not to do to make those enterprise-wide projects a success. The bad news is, implementing companies and consultancies have seldom incorporated this leading-practice project approach, and many, if not most, organizations had a pretty rough time of ERP implementation because they failed to do so.

It is worth noting that a majority of businesses still claim that they failed to get the business benefits that they had hoped from ERP implementations. This was seldom because the software platforms lacked functionality, but rather because organizations focused on implementing piecemeal, technical solutions, forgoing the difficult and controversial changes to long-established processes, reporting structures, and reward systems—and, too often, the organizations avoided taking on the even more contentious issues associated with worker activities (and often, therefore, positions) eliminated through automation.

Experience has now shown that most projects go wrong (or simply never really get off the ground) because the organization—and therefore the supporting consultancy and the software vendor—fails to take into account the fundamentally different nature of a true enterprise-wide transformation project from that of traditional software implementation. Typically, best intentions and great enthusiasm give way to multiple, overlapping initiatives and broad disagreement over what is in and out of scope, organizational quarrels over which initiatives should take priority, and frustration and bewilderment of executives who think it is all about simply implementing a software solution.[1]

GROUND RULES FOR AN E-PROCUREMENT PROJECT

With the upcoming era of e-procurement initiatives, the last thing the economy or organizations need is a *déjà vu* of those ERP struggles. Accordingly, there are certain ground rules that have been learned by organizations over the past five years that those involved in an enterprise-wide initiative should ignore at their own peril.

1. Ensure executive sponsorship and participation.
2. Make your e-procurement project integral to your overall e-business strategy.

3. Build a legitimate business case.

4. Set your guiding principles before you initiate the project.

5. Develop a strong program of change management.

6. Redesign your business processes before selecting software.

Executive Sponsorship and Participation

Because e-procurement will mean many things to many people (and nothing at all to some), it is dangerous to assume that the key leaders within your organization fully understand the goals, scope, and case for action behind the initiative. Lack of clarity around the business context and the failure to understand the strategic importance of an e-procurement initiative can result in a lack of momentum and support from your key organizational leaders. *If the executives themselves don't have a common understanding of the business need and the project approach, the project from the outset is in danger of degenerating into a battle over funding and resources, languishing, running long—or worst of all—resulting in a poorly integrated technical solution that does not take into account process and activity changes.* This means high cost and little business return.

It is still frustrating to see how often, despite the cost and strategic nature of these enterprise-wide projects, executives assume that their participation in planning, sponsoring, and actively driving the project forward is unnecessary. As we have learned from other enterprise-wide initiatives, unless the key organizational leadership (and this means the Chief Executive Officer, the Chief Operations Officer, the Chief Financial Officer, the Chief Procurement Officer, and the director of MIS) are actively involved from the onset of the project—and that means active not only in providing input in the early planning phases, but also continuously adding their support and sponsorship throughout the project—the tendency will be for the project to drift toward the strongest interest groups, to erupt in continuous debate over purpose and ownership, and to overrun in terms of time and budget.

Unfortunately, despite the almost universal claim by consultancies to provide a "full service" offering, very few e-procurement specialist consultants are comfortable working at this executive level— talking directly with the most senior executives in the organization in terms that are meaningful to executive non-specialists, arguing a business case, or developing a broader project that encompasses business process restructuring and change management. The reality is that, just as ERP systems were sold to the CIO and APS systems to the COO, e-procurement vendors and consultants will invariably target the manager one level below the director of procurement and drive the sales program from there.

The problem comes if the e-procurement initiative is seen as tactical and technical, and not strategic. It is therefore critical at the earliest planning stages of the initiative to provide a forum for all the key leaders to debate, define, and reach consensus on what it is they are trying to accomplish with an e-procurement initiative: what the project will entail, why the initiative is necessary, how it affects other current or planned initiatives, how long it will take, who will be involved, how much money it will cost, and what the expected return on investment will be.

Integrate E-Procurement Project with E-Business Strategy

It is becoming widely accepted that e-procurement should be seen as part of a company's overall e-business strategy, and therefore needs to be planned and managed as a single, company-wide initiative. Yet, it is still not uncommon today to find organizations approaching their company's broader e-business strategy through multiple, often conflicting and overlapping initiatives, with each initiative leader convinced that his or her project alone—a new Web page, an online central purchasing package, a decision support system—constitutes the most important e-business point of focus.

Even if, as will often be the case, the organization's overall e-business initiative itself is made up of many smaller but quite legitimate projects, these efforts need to be prioritized and coordinated. Web page development needs to be planned alongside changes in strategy to the broader order-fulfillment process. APS systems should be coordinated with ERP initiatives and tied into the procurement process. Those responsible for online marketing need to understand the effect that promises made to customers—in price, availability, or customization—will have on manufacturing, procurement, and the supply chain.

An approach that has usually proven to be successful in the past is to prioritize these various, interrelated projects, then design and implement them as a series of pilots within a single, all-encompassing e-business strategy. The criteria for prioritization may vary; you may decide to complete the easiest area first, to concentrate on the area where it is most important that you succeed, or to simply focus on the initiative where you can achieve the most benefit.

This same principle holds true even within the confines of the e-procurement initiative itself. Early decisions need to be made on

- Whether ORM should be the key area of focus
- Whether you wish to coordinate and integrate MRO with direct purchasing
- Whether you can make logical divisions between strategic and tactical commodities
- When and how you will go about consolidating suppliers
- What portions of the process should be restructured for "hands-free" efficiency
- What your new approval policy should be

Whatever the outcome of this prioritization effort, it is crucial that you avoid having multiple, uncoordinated, and competing initiatives.

A Legitimate Business Case

Much of the potential for organizational conflict can be reduced simply by getting early agreement on the likely costs and benefits of the e-procurement initiative. For those executives or leaders anywhere in the organization who still view procurement as bureaucratic, tactical, back-office work, making a legitimate business case will probably be essential to gaining meaningful support.

There are several key areas of cost/benefit that you should investigate carefully before proposing an e-procurement scenario—and certainly before approaching a software vendor. Not only will they help you gain sponsorship, but they will be invaluable in helping you to make critical decisions about implementation and software selection.

- **Analyze your purchasing process.** Understand what types of purchases you make, breaking down transactions by cost and volume. Can different materials be divided by their strategic or tactical nature, by their delivery time sensitivity, or by their importance to production schedules?

- **Document your transaction costs.** Try to calculate the amount of labor time spent by your purchasing employees on manual data entry, on filling out requisition forms, retyping purchase orders, sending faxes, and making confirmation telephone calls to suppliers. Understand how this varies between purchasing categories (ORM versus MRO) and between supplier groups. With direct purchasing, also figure in costs associated with holding excess safety stock. Some companies attempt to calculate lost opportunity costs, when purchasing specialists end up completing administrative work at the expense of critical supplier negotiations concerning discounting or extra-value services. In short, try to understand what your transaction costs amount to in real dollars.

■ **Complete a contract procurement analysis.** Examine your current purchasing contract process by completing an inventory on current procurement contracts held by your company with your various vendors. Look at numbers and types of contracts—travel, marketing, office supplies, MRO—that you have currently. Are they held centrally, or are these contracts made unilaterally by different departments? Do these contracts conflict or vary widely among vendor groups, materials, or departments?

■ **Create an inventory of RFPs.** Carry out a similar analysis on your current tendering process. Understand if Request for Proposals (RFTs and RFIs) vary greatly between departments or materials and if they follow similar leading-practice or industry standards.

■ **Create an inventory of vendors.** Try to document what suppliers get what percentages of your purchasing budget, and rate them in terms of how well they have performed historically and by their strengths and weaknesses.

■ **Review your current and future payment strategy options.** Are you currently using corporate purchasing cards? If not, what options might you have? If so, can they provide the level of service that you anticipate for your e-procurement solution?

Those executives focused on the bottom line may quite justifiably balk at the idea of the "soft costs" that are thrown around so often by software vendors and the optimistic side of the business press. Thus, savings such as "reduced time spent on purchase order and invoice reconciliation" or those derived from many different functional areas within the organization may not be accepted at face value. Similar skepticism may arise with vague ideas about "shifting resources to strategic sourcing." As valid as this might be, it is something still far too subjective to calculate for bottom line costs or savings. Therefore, set the ground rules on all of this up front with executives, and decide beforehand if you need to have an objective ROI in order to justify moving forward. Many veterans of such projects warn of the dangers of avoiding the issue of ROI, explaining that either the organizational leaders accept the need for e-procurement intuitively, or you need to design an ROI scheme that takes into account both hard and soft savings.

Guiding Principles

It is also important to get agreement among your key organizational leaders on certain guiding principles that will govern the approach and outcome of the e-procurement initiative. Will you be making changes to just tactical ORM goods, or will your project include direct materials? Is outsourcing an option? What sort of levels of independence and "empowerment" with purchasing do you hope to achieve? The more concrete and measurable these guidelines are, the more valuable they will be to those working on the project in the future.

One critical area of concern that should be dealt with and decided on by the key organizational leaders is what to do about "displaced staff"—those in the procurement process whose primary activities will be eliminated by changes to the process or by implementing a system. As we learned from ERP implementations, it can be particularly difficult for the purchasing group to lead the effort and yet ask the very people who understand the process best to both create an improved process and to eliminate their own jobs at the same instant. The guiding principles governing how these displaced workers will be treated can make a huge difference when asking for support and subject matter expertise, and far too many companies do not have the leadership or presence of mind to make clear policy decisions in this area. The answer seems to be to develop a clear policy based on a strong business case and a compassionate approach to retraining and redeployment, communicate it openly to all levels in the organization, and then adhere to it rigorously.

Strong Change Management Program

As we have already seen, e-procurement means significant changes to the way that your organization orders, approves, and receives products. Equally important will be a completely new emphasis, for most companies, on tactical and strategic buying, with a significant change to roles, responsibilities, and reporting lines for those involved.

Accordingly, manual work, except on a rare "exception-only" basis, will completely disappear, and so will the jobs of those currently doing data entry and reconciliation tasks. As their work shifts from transactional to strategic work, remember that long-time purchasing employees may worry (quite rightly) that they do not have the skills that will allow them to transfer easily into this new strategic world. After all, it can be quite a transition from paper-based order management to the more strategic world of analysis and supplier negotiations and management.

As a procurement officer deep in an e-procurement project recently remarked, "I like the supplier savings here, but I don't plan to be one of the transactional savings."[2]

There are many things that you can do to ensure that a strong program of change management is in place in order to help ease the transition for employees and the company as a whole. These include making certain that key executives understand and agree on the goals, approach, and timing of the project, and that the project is coordinated and managed through a strong, participative project management office that provides structure, clarity, integration, and direction. It is also important, as we have said, to make certain that implications on changes to process and work activities are formally captured through an implications analysis. Finally, and possibly most important of all, the entire change project must be formally managed according to an agreed-upon change transition plan, which includes a comprehensive, executive-led communication plan and an employee participation program that ensures enthusiasm and "buy-in" broadly throughout the organization. (All of this is discussed in much greater detail in Chapter 14.)

Redesign Business Processes

Two key principles behind a successful e-procurement initiative are that it must be enterprise-wide and it must be founded on changes to strategy and process, not simply on technology. Although it has now become accepted wisdom, it is worth repeating, because it has never been more valid than it is today with enterprise-wide e-procurement implementations.

"Automating a mess yields an automated mess," explains John Corini of Deloitte Consulting's e-business practice. "The net change in these cases is the substitution of an inbox full of paper requisitions with an email-box full of electronic requisitions."[3]

Yet, despite all we have learned over the past five years about implementing ERP, far too often e-procurement projects are still being sponsored and controlled by technical consultants and MIS staff, and focus more on implementation of technology than on achieving overall business benefits.

In this golden era of marketing, consultancies almost universally claim that they provide a full-service e-procurement solution, but in reality, the vast majority of consultancies in this market space have a strong technical bias. But enterprise-wide, e-procurement implementation—including the necessary changes to business processes—is something very different from catalog management or portal provision. Enterprise-wide process redesign, working with senior executives to clarify operational strategy, and implementing complex change programs, are all services seen as foreign and dangerous ground to most consultancies. Uncomfortable dealing with high liability and high ambiguity, most consultants (and internal project employees) quite justifiably prefer the safer ground of well-defined, cleanly scoped projects limited to implementation of software modules. *Yet, unless those process changes are explicitly identified and made with a targeted change program, the functionality and therefore the value of the software (as far too many companies have discovered after poor implementations of ERP systems) will be seriously limited.*

In keeping with lessons learned that extend back to the basic concepts of business process reengineering (remember the seminal article by Hammer and Champy, "Don't Automate, Obliterate"), most companies that have been through an e-procurement project recommend analyzing the procurement process and fundamentally remapping how you plan to do the process based upon a paperless approach, sometimes known as a *hands-free* model. This means getting together with procurement specialists and suppliers and restructuring the entire purchasing process—first on paper and then live—so that there is minimal human intervention, and only on an exceptional basis for items of critical importance or that require special negotiations or handling. At the heart of this exception-only philosophy are changes to the approvals process, eliminating the multiple financial and technical sign-offs that so often does little to eliminate maverick buying or waste, and usually only slows down the purchasing process and adds to overall costs. An underlying principle behind electronic procurement is that employees are free to purchase as necessary within prescribed criteria, and that—as long as there is an accurate audit trail for purchases—approvals are not automated; they are eliminated altogether.

Working through this exercise helps to highlight the advantages of a fully automated system and can help you to go a long way toward documenting the likely time savings and cost benefits of an e-procurement initiative. Many find that even if they do not immediately move toward a system installation, the hands-free process mapping itself helps them to fundamentally rethink their antiquated, over-audited approach to procurement. It also provides a good opportunity to take a "first cut" at the implications analysis, so that you can develop an early sense of the ways in which employees will be affected.

OTHER KEY ISSUES TO CONSIDER BEFORE STARTING

Integration Issues

Because of the time, resources, and money associated with the effort, opinion varies as to whether back-end systems integration should take place before or after the initial e-procurement implementation. Some suggest that a company should start by achieving cost savings and supplier consolidation first.

"There is a need for ERP integration if you are a big company and you want to pass that purchase order from the ERP system to the e-procurement system," contends Mikko Talsi, ICL's director of B2B e-commerce. "But the reason for doing e-procurement in the first place is for cost savings from supplier consolidation and managing maverick buying."

"Don't start by hooking up ERP," he advises. "Start by using it as an ordering channel; and then move on to considering how you can integrate it into your back-end system. If you start with a big ERP integration, you might not see the return on investment, because your company and needs may change before you achieve it."[4]

A contrary school of thought contends that true business efficiency only comes from seamless interconnectivity with back-end systems, and therefore the first phase of an e-procurement project may be—particularly for mission-critical direct inventory and supply chain—to create the internal links with the ERP systems. As we have seen too often, leaving behind the business benefit changes may mean they are never achieved, because starting up a new project after an exhausting effort can be risky. Whichever strategy is best for your company, it is important to get agreement early among your executive sponsors, and guidance on project scope should be clearly captured in your guiding principles.

Involving Suppliers and Vendors

"Supplier participation is no less critical to the successful implementation of any e-procurement solution," notes John Corini of Deloitte Consulting. "Without this participation, the software is useless. Few experiences are more disheartening than to finally overcome your own company's fear of electronic commerce only to run into resistance on the supplier side."[5]

One problem is that very often, small or medium-sized vendors simply have little IT functionality or expertise. Remember that the vast majority of suppliers still typically have little more than an Internet Web page, describing themselves and their basic services or product lines. Even large suppliers often do not see this type of IT as a core competency and lack the resources to do sophisticated, time-consuming, and often costly electronic catalog maintenance. E-procurement for them may seem to involve enormous investment and disruption with little visible return.

There are many examples of the dangers of overestimating a supplier's willingness and ability to make these dramatic leaps onto the Internet. "We tremendously underestimated the effort involved in getting catalogs online," explained one major oil company executive. "Our plan had been to get 40 to 50 implemented within the first six months. By the end of that period, all we had gotten online were two."[6]

After all, there is no point forcing your valued suppliers to overcommit and ultimately risk under-delivery, simply because expectations were missed or badly communicated at the outset of the project. Many suppliers express fears of an impersonal e-procurement process that strips them of their competitive advantage. And, after all, as the head of one of the largest online trading communities recently confessed, one of the unstated aims of any exchange is to "beat the hell out of suppliers."

Accordingly, although this will probably not be the case for the large ORM distributors, for small or niche materials suppliers it can be important to involve them in your deliberations from the outset, sharing with them the fundamentals of the business case. *For those suppliers outside of the spot-market or auction strategy, vendors that remain as your preferred partners need to appreciate that you are not simply trying to reduce costs internally at their expense, but are willing to respond to added value or trusted vendor status from them.* Including these suppliers in early justification and design meetings can help, as can a willingness to subsidize them during the transition with resources or implementation support. Equally, because you cannot involve all your suppliers in the e-procurement planning process, it may be necessary to identify only key supplier partnerships early on. This again argues the case for completing your purchasing and vendor analyses first.

The lesson seems to be clear: Decide who your key suppliers should be and include them as an integral part of your e-procurement project, tying them into clear and attainable milestones and building them directly into your change management plan.

Bringing in Consultants

One of the most important decisions for the steering committee and project leaders will be deciding what sort of help your organization will need from outside partners, and to whom you should turn, and when. Because of the enormous cost and disruption of ERP implementations, some larger companies have moved toward using consultants only when absolutely necessary—for niche areas such as security or XML support and of course for the software implementation itself. Consider, however, the advice and expertise that will be necessary—wherever obtained—for an e-procurement project:

- Leading-practice procurement strategies
- Outsourcing versus in-house strategy advice
- Leading operational-level e-procurement practices
- Process mapping and redesign
- Change management
- Program and project management
- Financial and payment services support for integration with in-house financials, for payment processing, and for third-party financial services support
- Assessment of and participation in auctions, exchanges, and trading communities
- Technical architecture and design

- Data management
- Security
- Specialist services such as catalog content management and buyer and supplier systems administration
- Advisory and help desk support for desktop requisitioning
- Technical and new business process training
- Knowledge management, data mining, and decision support systems and processes
- Supply chain management, supplier management, and strategic sourcing
- Expertise in XML, Extended Application Integration (EAI), and system-to-system integration
- Business case justification and performance measurement

These types of skills, unfortunately, are not always going to be available from within a company's employee ranks. Some organizations have been able to utilize the internal project management skills of project leaders and team members who have dedicated the past several years to implementing their ERP systems, but in reality, very few companies have the internal expertise, confidence, or capacity to venture into this type of project without the help of consultants. Despite the shortcomings of many consultancies, there are still sound reasons for turning to outside help.

First of all, of course, there is expertise needed for e-procurement software implementation, but also for strategy, procurement, leading practices, business process redesign, project management, legacy systems integration, and change management. In fact, these areas are just as important as the technical capacity to implement or integrate. Too often, companies believe that they can use their own people to reengineer processes and implement organizational change but although their input is valuable, it is essential to get new ideas, and these almost invariably come from benchmarking or lessons learned brought in by a third-party specialist. It is important to keep in mind that this type of procurement process and business transformation expertise is usually not found in the software vendor, technical support, or IT staff.

The second reason for turning externally for help is simply the toll of such projects on internal resources. Companies need to keep their procurement and IT departments running, and even strong levels of participation on the core team alone will stretch good employees to their limits. Quite apart from the design work itself, these e-procurement projects will require extensive discussions with suppliers and time-consuming hours spent in content management and data administration (developing and taking down business policies, supplier profiles, end-user information, and so on).

The third reason for turning to outside support is to take advantage of a strong third party's relative political independence. Although you will often still need to grapple with the "not invented here" syndrome, and many company executives will balk at the idea of consultancies doing more than simply fulfilling basic "staff augmentation" services, if you can find a strong management consultancy with one or two experienced consultants who will help to advise and guide the project and the executives in key nontechnical areas (business change and project management is seldom a concern to the software vendors themselves), they can be well worth the cost.

NEW RESPONSIBILITIES FOR CONSULTANCIES

It is interesting to reflect that only two years ago, many industry watchers and partners in the large consultancy firms were beginning to wonder where, as an industry, management consulting was going. Lay-offs, particularly in the weakening ERP sector, had already begun. The two key growth areas—complexity and knowledge management—had failed to produce the lengthy and lucrative projects found in the quickly evaporating ERP market, and there seemed nothing ahead except piecemeal systems upgrade work and minor business process improvement projects to sustain an industry bloated with thousands of young generalists and heads-down technical specialists. Then, to everyone's relief and to many consultancies' total surprise, e-business in all its forms exploded onto the business scene.[7]

The very fact that nearly every consultancy now markets itself as "leading" and "thoroughly experienced" practitioners of e-business should be a cause for concern. After all, taken up by the sheer energy of the media blitz surrounding e-business, it is easy to forget that only three years ago, the Internet, online sales, e-procurement portals, and online trading communities and auctions were totally alien to most consultancies' experience.

Yet, as nearly every consultancy attempts—through ever-creative marketing—to convince customers that they are uniquely qualified to help an organization with creating and implementing an e-business strategy and infrastructure, it is important to realize that transforming an organization from a bricks-and-mortar business to an extended, electronically integrated enterprise is as revolutionary as the nature of e-business itself, and in many ways far more difficult than implementing an ERP system. It is certainly more complex than simply creating a Web page or browser. Of course, the chickens are just now coming home to roost, and at the time of press, the share prices of the top 15 listed Internet consultancies have dropped as much as 90% since their phenomenal highs during the dotcom craze. They have laid off, as an industry group, more than 3,000 employees, and more are likely to go in the near term. There are many lessons to be learned (one is, don't bet your company on fees to be repaid by insolvent dotcom start ups).

In order to help organizations successfully make this transition to e-procurement, consultancies will need to provide sophisticated, impartial, well-informed advice, and will need to take on new levels of responsibility for their recommendations. In short, they need to do what they failed to do with ERP. Unfortunately, as many organizations are already finding out, despite the fact that nearly every consultancy boasts the ability to provide a full-service e-business offering, in most cases these consultancies are severely overselling themselves. *Moreover, the industry (and in fact the economy as a whole) is woefully short on the specific skills in e-procurement software implementation and large-scale transition change management that are now necessary in order to help companies make this important transition.* The majority have only one or two areas of specialty focus and often a limited capacity to advise on or implement even a basic level of business process or organizational change. Unfortunately, the software providers themselves, although they know their products well, seldom will enter into the realm of advice at the level required to rethink and optimize an entire procurement process.

In fact, the complexities involved in designing and implementing an e-procurement strategy effectively is something for which the vast majority of consultancies simply are not prepared. This is something that every client should think about and economists should note, because the success of individual businesses, and ultimately, the increases in productivity necessary to sustain our current level of growth in the manufacturing area and in the economy as a whole is dependent in no small way upon the ability of consultancies to help organizations through this challenging transformation.

Accordingly, there are several basic things that you can do to help mitigate the risk that comes from overdependency on consultants.

■ Make certain that you do not cede overall responsibility for the success of the project to any one consultancy. Even if a large and ambitious consultancy promises to be the "general contractor" for the initiative (often a good idea), there is no substitute for client-sponsored program management supported by a well-informed and involved executive steering committee. Too often, after a brief enthusiastic blessing of the project, executives retreat from active participation, leaving a well-intentioned but politically less powerful project manager to run with the project and deal with the many risk and change issues that will arise. Invariably problems develop that are beyond the project manager's power to resolve, leaving them to try to keep the issues under wraps or fearfully bringing one-off issues for resolution back to an ill-informed and impatient executive group.

■ Many of the most successful projects have therefore appointed a strong internal program manager, who, as the deputy to the CEO, is seen as the person responsible (after the CEO) for the success of the overall initiative. Remember that program management skills (enterprise-wide management of multiple projects) are often very different from project management skills (focused on the success of one separable segment—a project—of the overall initiative) and require a different personality and a different level of political clout. A program manager should be able to garner wide support within the organization and have the presence to engage other executives on equal terms.

■ Give both technical and business process and change aspects of the program equal weight by appointing technical and nontechnical project managers who report directly to the overall program manager. The technical project manager should be responsible for all MIS-related matters; the nontechnical project manager should oversee all business process and change management initiatives. Though it is often valuable to also have outside consultants with "shadow" positions in these areas, these two key people should be from your own company and should be responsible for resolving inter-consultancy conflicts and for driving the project forward in a balanced way. They will be the operational-level managers of the entire program.

- Finally, make certain that you come to agreement with the outside consultants early on as to a plan for integrating their activities with those of the many other participants involved. There will be a scramble between any consultants worth their salt for control over key aspects of the project. Help them to clearly outline their proposed approach, including activities and named resources, before you begin the project. Clarity as to specific roles, responsibilities and deliverables is essential.

The fact is, as promising and revolutionary as e-procurement is, it will mean new challenges to businesses and consultancies alike. In order to avoid the pitfalls of the ERP era, consultancies will have to truly provide—rather than just pay lip service to—a full solution, or else learn to collaborate with other specialty and niche providers. Because e-procurement initiatives by their nature are enterprise-wide and dependent upon critical changes to business processes, consultancies will need to develop the ability to integrate business process and change management into their offerings much more successfully than they have in the past.

Client organizations, for their part, will have to learn to take more responsibility for the overall success of projects, helping to provide a collaborative forum for multiple consultants without ceding full authority to any single group. Because of the strategic nature of e-business (particularly with direct materials), and because of the inability of most consultancies to provide a full-service offering, it is likely that organizations will find themselves increasingly taking on a much more active role as program managers and coordinators. This, when combined up front with honesty and clarity from consultancies on what services they can and cannot provide, will make a client's new-found role as catalyst and consultant manager much easier and more successful.

Finally, don't forget the lessons of the past and allow your e-business project to once again drift toward a purely technical implementation. One of the unavoidable facts of modern business life is that business, change management, and technical specialists seldom work and play well together (even within the same consulting firm, let alone among competing ones). Civil war within your project can be best avoided by structuring a project approach that retains program management authority internally and gives equal weight to both technical implementation and business change.

After all, neither side—consultants or clients—can afford a *déjà vu* of ERP.

ENDNOTES

1. Neef, Dale, "Consultants Can't Solve All Your E-Business Problems," *Handbook of Business Strategy,* (New York: Faulkner & Gray, 2000), p. 7.
2. Corini, John, "Integrating e-Procurement and Strategic Sourcing," *Supply Chain Management Review,* March 2000, p. 7.
3. Corini, John, "Integrating e-Procurement and Strategic Sourcing," *Supply Chain Management Review,* March 2000, p. 4.
4. McDonald, Sheila, "Top Story: B2B Hits the Trenches," *Electric-News.net,* April 28, 2000, p. 3.
5. Corini, John, "Integrating e-Procurement and Strategic Sourcing," *Supply Chain Management Review,* March 2000, p. 3.
6. Corini, John, "Integrating e-Procurement and Strategic Sourcing," *Supply Chain Management Review,* March 2000, p. 4.
7. Parts of the text on the following pages is excerpted by permission from two recent articles: Neef, Dale, "Consultants Can't Solve All Your E-Business Problems, Handbook of Business Strategy," in *2001 Handbook of Business Strategy* (Thomson Financial Media, 2001), pp. 63–72; and Neef, Dale, "Hiring an E-Team," *Business Strategy,* November/December 2000, pp. 17–21.

Structuring the Project: Phases of an Enterprise-wide E-Procurement Initiative

Objective

The way in which you structure your enterprise-wide e-procurement initiative will have a profound effect on the results. There are several key things to be considered:

- It is important to set your e-procurement initiative within the company's overall e-strategy.

- Careful project planning and management, including coordinating the e-procurement initiative with other ongoing company initiatives, is essential.

- It is important that you integrate an implications analysis that captures changes to business processes, job activities, and personnel policies directly into your implementation project.

- Use well thought-out criteria when making your system selection.

Most companies by now have had some experience with large and complex IT or business restructuring initiatives, and will be familiar with

There are distinct phases of an enterprise-wide project. Each is important, and none of them should be missed.

the basic framework of enterprise-wide projects. However, there are some important aspects of the project approach—involving suppliers, building the business case, developing scoring criteria for software platform selection—that are unique to an e-procurement initiative.

To begin with, let's review the key phases of an enterprise-wide e-procurement project, shown in Figure 12.1.

STRATEGY PHASE

Although many companies have established annual retreats and strategic planning days to help executive teams develop their marketing strategy (and therefore often mistakenly believe that they have already done the "strategic planning stuff"), it is important that before beginning any major enterprise-wide e-procurement initiative, the key organizational leaders convene to discuss and agree on the way forward. Usually completed in a workshop setting with 10 to 12 key organizational leaders attending—who should be all company officers, including the CEO—this forum provides an opportunity for the executive group to become educated on the many aspects of e-procurement; to debate and agree on the case for action; to consider the need for business process restructuring, supplier involvement, and risk and change management; and to reach consensus on the basic scope of the project, including cost, resources, and timescales.

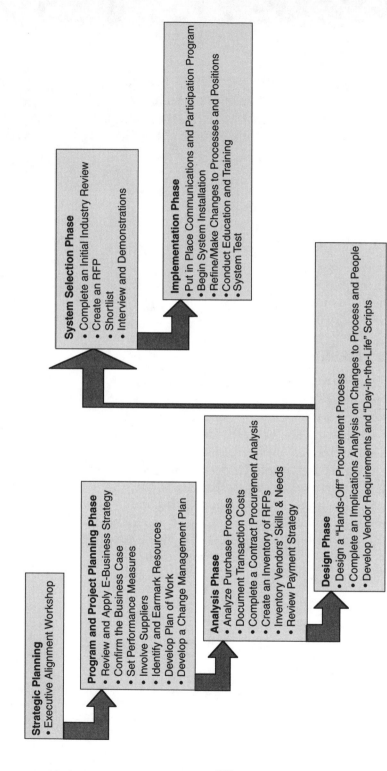

Figure 12.1 Key phases of an enterprise-wide e-procurement project.

The strategic alignment workshop (which is described in much more detail in Chapter 13) should begin by examining the key issues facing your company over the next one to three years, and should include discussion and agreement on

- The core competency and focus of the company over the next few years
- How your products and services may change during that time
- Key ways in which you will differentiate your products or services from those of your competitors
- Future markets and possible growth, scale, and geography considerations
- Critical changes occurring in terms of customer support, standards, or expectations of quality
- Issues concerning procurement of ORM, MRO, and direct goods, including inefficiencies, lack of leverage, maverick buying, and lack of compliance
- The changing nature of your relationship with vendors and partners, and how these relationships may be affected by e-procurement and strategic sourcing
- How e-procurement plans might affect the supply chain: purchasing, inventory management, supplier management, logistics, and product design
- Business systems support architecture requirements (AR, AP, GL, performance tracking, reporting)
- Coordinating your own, and competing with other ongoing, planned initiatives
- Prioritization, project risks, and change management issues
- Project planning, including timescales, resources, and budgeting

Ultimately, the output from the workshop becomes a foundation-planning document that serves as a "constitution" for your company's e-procurement project. *But the real value of this early strategic planning comes from providing a forum for discussing and clarifying the scope and goals of the project, gaining consensus at the executive level on all major project issues, and providing those involved—now and in the future— with a clear understanding of why the project is necessary, what you are trying to achieve, and how you believe it should be done.*

Far too often, this type of strategic workshop approach is seen as unnecessary or simply too uncomfortable for the executive team, who often have long-running grievances that they fear may erupt into open conflict. Probably 8 out of 10 projects instead drop immediately to the tactical level, with responsibility for moving straight to software selection being given to a small team from IT and procurement. This invariably means that the e-procurement project is seen as little more than a technology implementation, without the strategic context, focus, or direction necessary to ensure a successful outcome.

It is important for project change management that this executive group continues to participate in the process as an active steering committee. This will help to keep them informed about—and engaged in—the project. It is also better for them and their employees if these same organizational leaders are responsible for communication and sponsorship of the project within their sphere of influence.

PROGRAM AND PROJECT PLANNING

Based on the same premise as the need to ensure clarity and consensus around the e-procurement initiative, the planning phase drops the level of discussion from the strategic to the operational and begins to develop a detailed program plan for the project. Accordingly, the planning phase is usually conducted in a similar workshop setting—to gain the same level of interactive, multifunction discussion and consensus-building—but the attendees are operational-level managers and specialists (from purchasing, finance, MIS, manufacturing, etc.) who know the current procurement process well. This is essentially where the specialists will put the "meat on the bones" of the project initiated by the executive alignment workshop. Key steps, which we will examine individually, include:

- Reviewing the company's strategic direction, guiding principles, and project goals
- Reconfirming and developing the case for action
- Setting target performance measures
- Exploring the supplier side
- Examining critical areas of concern and earmarking resources
- Completing a project readiness assessment and developing a plan of work

Strategic Direction, Guiding Principles, and Project Goals

To begin the session, a review of the results of the executive strategic alignment workshop will help the operational-level managers to understand the nature, scope, and need for the project—at least as seen by the executive team. One of the most important aspects of project success is for everyone involved from the start to know precisely what they are hoping to achieve, and it is well worth the time to debate and agree on what the overall goals of the project are, how success will be measured, what functional areas are included or excluded, and when the project needs to be completed. As the operational managers begin to bring detail to the project, it will be immediately obvious why the executive alignment workshop was necessary. Nothing can be more frustrating for the planning team or the executives if key guiding principles and scoping intentions are not clearly defined first by the executives, and then spelled out in their "constitution."

The Case for Action

In order to get to the next level of clarity and agreement, the group will want to examine their views of the compelling issues that gave rise to the e-procurement project, and to develop a consensus as to why the organization must change the current way of procuring goods and why those changes need to occur at this time. A fair level of skepticism is good, but if not everyone agrees on the need for change and the goals and scope of the project, it is important that those points are made and resolved before the initiative is taken any further. Again, clarity and consensus at the beginning of these projects helps to eliminate many of the risks associated with cross-functional, enterprise-wide initiatives that overlap managerial territories and personal domains.

The level of exchange and discussion will be much more detailed than the sweeping assertions usually made at the executive level, and as each key area of improvement—process efficiencies, leverage, and compliance—is examined, the team should quickly be able to develop a plan for verifying the business case.

Target Performance Measures

In order to avoid anecdotal-level discussions and disagreements, the planning group will need to identify some meaningful indicators of performance, which will bring as much objectivity as possible to the project. These might include

- Lost discount costs
- Overall labor costs
- Time spent in routine ORM requisitioning
- Time and labor dedicated to working with suppliers
- Numbers of suppliers

- Time spent rekeying data
- Average approval wait-time
- Amount and cost of maverick buying

Using these indicators, the next step is to set target performance measures for the procurement process that will help to actually measure the success of the initiative. The group will need to think carefully about these measurements. The measurements must be true indicators of performance, and the group will want to be certain that attaining these target levels will actually result in meaningful improvements in the overall effectiveness of both the procurement function and the organization as a whole. Most likely, the executive team has endorsed the project based on a combination of partially understood statistics, anecdotal information on inefficiencies, or just on intuition. Putting some objective numbers to the business case will help gain clarity and cement support, and is in itself a revealing exercise in exploring the pros and cons of changing the current process and gauging the value of a shift toward electronic procurement.

The Supplier Side

Many companies have found that an e-procurement initiative provides a unique opportunity to review their entire relationship with suppliers. During the planning phase, the group should decide if their purchasing activities fall naturally into categories—strategic or tactical, mission-critical or support, vendor-dependent or widely available, and so on. This sort of criteria can be used to help categorize the usually disparate supplier base, providing an opportunity to begin the high-level strategic sourcing exercises that most companies wish to do but never find the time to complete.

It also provides an opportunity to start tentative discussions with key suppliers, and to assess their level of willingness to support a shift toward e-procurement. Chances are that many of your suppliers are only too willing to support your organization in that change, but may have no clear idea what is expected of them—how to participate, what changes they will need to make, or how much it will cost them. If your project is limited to ORM and desktop requisitioning, most large wholesale suppliers will already be well prepared to provide electronic catalogs, either directly to you or to your chosen ASP. Many will already have at least rudimentary portal and e-purchasing capabilities. MRO goods often involve specialist and smaller suppliers, and these companies may eventually need to participate actively in your design workshops. It is important to first make certain that key suppliers have the information and assistance necessary to ramp up their efforts on the same timescale as your own, and then make certain that you don't begin to develop a software solution that excludes key suppliers because it is incompatible with their IT competency levels or their ability to restructure themselves in line with your plans.

Resources and Critical Areas of Concern

During this early planning phase, the group will want to review the major activities within the full procurement process—indirect or direct—at a very high level and agree on what resources will be needed to accurately understand these key activity areas—supplier management, order taking, requisitioning, reconciliation, accounts payable, receiving, inventory management, MIS—and how they will be affected by a shift to e-procurement. This means enlisting the help of some of the most knowledgeable people in the organization to form a "core team" and earmarking a number of experts to help on specific issues. Unfortunately, these are normally the same people who keep the organization running on a daily basis, so it is important to begin to plan early for their participation. That means specifically contacting the specialists, their managers, and directors, and getting their consent and assistance in planning and coordinating schedules.

Even at this early stage of the project, you are likely to encounter the first hints of project change management issues, as managers resist handing over resources, and rivals of the specialists being sought contend that they should be consulted also—or instead of—those chosen for the core team. In fact, selection of core team or workshop participants sometimes requires significant political finesse. It is the first test of the sponsoring executive's dedication to the project, and he or she may need to be asked to intercede in order to guarantee the necessary resources. Often, it is necessary to create secondary workshops to inform and include colleagues, and in order to demonstrate that there is nothing "secret" or exclusive about the e-procurement design process, and that their opinions, too, are valued.

In fact, many companies at this point will also begin planning for a broad series of employee "input workshops" that, conducted in the first few weeks of the analysis phase, have a twofold effect. First, these workshops are a good forum for soliciting valuable suggestions on how to improve the process from the employees who are closest to, and most knowledgeable about, the work on a day-to-day basis. Second, these workshops serve as a forum for discussion and communication of the business case and project goals, and help employees to understand why the project is necessary and why their support is so valuable. *Employee input workshops require a good deal of time and effort, but have been shown time and time again on enterprise-wide change projects to be extremely effective in helping to consolidate employee buy-in.* During the planning phase, these resources need to be identified and secured, and a full project plan, including calendars, needs to be produced.

If the program manager has not yet been selected, she or he should be appointed (ideally, this should be someone who participated in the executive alignment workshop). It is important not only that the program manager is involved in these early formative discussions, but also that she or he now take the lead as the project "champion," with all the sponsorship and communication responsibilities that that role entails. The importance of having a project champion can hardly be overstressed. There is nothing more critical to the success of the initiative than a well-respected and fully engaged project champion (discussed further in Chapter 14).

Moreover, it is important that, under the direction of the overall program manager, department-level process champions be identified as "ambassadors" for communicating and supporting the goals of the project. A detailed, full-project plan should be developed with clear and consistent messages for the employees generally, and the champions should work with the nontechnical project manager (see Chapter 14) to create an effective communication plan. It seems a bit corny, but in fact, enthusiasm is still (next to good project planning and management) the most important tool that a company can use in affecting change in an organization.

Project Readiness Assessment and a Plan of Work

As a final step to the workshops, and as a result of the entire planning phase, a detailed plan of work needs to be agreed on with all the relevant stakeholders, which includes the project plan, timelines, milestones, resource needs, cost estimates, and expected deliverables. It is a lot of work, but necessary in order to clearly understand and gain broad agreement on project scope, and to identify and confirm participation and support from those involved with or affected by the project.

ANALYSIS AND DESIGN PHASES

During the analysis and design phases, the project finally shifts from planning to doing, and with a well thought-out and endorsed project plan in hand, the organization can now begin to analyze and redesign the procurement process. There are normally several areas of focus.

Collecting Information to Confirm the Business Case

Apart from the cost/benefit analysis on the current process, remember also that total project costs will be much greater than those associated with simply purchasing and implementing a system. Consulting, additional software, integration with legacy systems—in other words, total implementation costs—will run normally at levels from 5 to 10 times the cost of the software platform alone. And although ORM and most aspects of MRO may be fairly straightforward in terms of process design, direct procurement will be a major undertaking, involving changes to nearly every process and system in your entire supply chain. It is therefore usually worthwhile benchmarking total costs, when possible.

It is important that realistic expectations for total cost are set at the outset. If price expectations are set too low, executives can suffer "sticker shock" and be tempted to declare victory after phase one, without getting the true business benefits that require a larger and longer-term investment.

Confirming Supplier Support and Compatibility Levels

As we have seen, it is important to make certain that you design your e-procurement process with present and future supplier needs and capabilities in mind. This is particularly true if you have not kept up with a strong program of supplier consolidation and are unaware of their strategies or current transition programs. It is important to determine early on how many of your key suppliers are ready to take the leap toward electronic connections via the Internet, and to also know how many, if any, are currently developing similar collaborations with other buying companies. Do they have EDI at present, and if so, what is their plan for migrating to XML? Many large or specialist industry suppliers may already be planning to participate in vertical industry e-markets, and therefore may be already wondering how to provide electronic catalogs, either directly or through that industry portal.

Redesigning Business Processes

Redesigning business processes involves many workshops and detailed process-mapping sessions, and along with a sense of perspective (and humor), practitioners should be careful to keep several broad principles in mind:

- Use automation, whenever possible, with the view of minimizing human intervention (create a hands-off procurement process).

- Shift the responsibility for ORM goods purchasing, whenever possible, to the users' desktops.

- Make the process exception only by rethinking approval criteria.

- If both technical and financial approvals are necessary, make these happen on parallel and simultaneous paths.

- Reduce one-off product purchases to a minimum.

- Introduce data only once, at source, and make that data available to parties that require it simultaneously (suppliers, central purchasing, the employee-buyer, accounts payable, etc.).

- Reexamine and clearly define all roles and responsibilities from buyer through supplier.

Completing an Implications Analysis on Changes to Activities and Employee Jobs

One of the most often neglected, but easily completed, portions of the project is the implications analysis. This analysis is completed by the design workgroups, either during initial design or in some cases as late as software implementation, depending on approach. The implications analysis simply records the changes between the current state and the future state of the process, but focuses specifically on the work activities that will be changed or eliminated. For example, if the purchase order is no longer typed by hand but done automatically by the system, the team captures the fact that those specific manual production activities will no longer exist. As the team members work their way through the entire procurement process at activity level, they build up a significant profile of the changes to employees' future work activities.

By reducing the process to an activity level and then comparing manual with system-based approaches, this exercise provides a much more accurate and detailed understanding of what a company is trying to achieve with the new system, allowing the design team to make detailed system adjustments before implementation, or, alternatively, helping them to shift the company toward accepting built-in leading practices that are inherent to the software. Equally important, this approach provides an instant picture of the relative gap between the current and future ways that employees will work—no more faxing, or no more reconciliation of the invoice and the purchase order—down to the specific activity that will be eliminated. The steps of the implications analysis include

- Identifying changes in work (at activity, process, and unit level)

- Understanding what will not be done in the future

- Noting what changes in order, omission, and so on will require major organizational or structural changes (altered reporting lines, new decision-making responsibilities, etc.)

- Identifying skill changes necessary for current employees to complete the new activities

- Mapping of the future workforce (at skill level only, not by name) against the current procurement workforce in terms of what is done and who does it

Technical and process teams often worry that noting down specific activities and jobs that will be eliminated because of automation will cause too much political disruption to the project and within the company. They rightly appreciate the amount of resistance and concern that occurs when it becomes widely known that specific positions associated with the procurement process will be combined or eliminated. And yet, as with ERP, unless those activities—and therefore positions—are eliminated, the system's value is greatly reduced. *Employees will probably know, or at least suspect, that these types of positions are at risk anyway, and it is both unfeasible and unwise (as some consultancies still advocate) to try to make the design team's deliberations a secret.*

I once was called in to help with a large company project where the design team members had sequestered themselves away in several conference rooms; on the doors, they had hung hand-made signs depicting skull and crossbones with warnings of "Confidential Material" and "No Entry." Within weeks, the employee population was rife with rumors of wholesale layoffs and staff cuts, fueled by the total lack of a communication plan and the exclusive and clandestine airs of the project teams. After several "tell-us-or-else" demands were made to management, the CEO finally agreed to a rather enfeebled effort to explain that it was only an IT system. Unprepared, the CEO was trapped into admitting that the aim was, in part, to eliminate labor. Unable to put forward a convincing business case, afraid to pledge openness, and having given no thought to a personnel transition plan, the management team simply pledged that no job changes would be made, thereby undermining the entire point of a multimillion dollar software implementation.

The lesson, then, is that it is important to understand the likely implications on process and people as soon as possible, to develop a change transition plan, create project champions to promote the initiative and to communicate openly, and to elicit broad employee participation and input through employee workshops. Above all, employees should understand that they are genuinely responsible for the success of the e-procurement, and should be encouraged, as much as possible, to take "ownership" of that success themselves.

SYSTEM SELECTION PHASE

There are many good books on system selection techniques that can explain in detail how to develop your software requirements and "scripts" for vendor demonstrations, but it is worth noting that because of the volatile nature of the e-procurement software industry and marketplace just now, the scoring criteria for an e-procurement project should include several key areas of emphasis: cost, functionality, and integration and interoperability.

Cost

Although Gartner Group, confident of the potential returns of an e-procurement project, contends that an organization should expect an ROI to be justified in two years,[1] it is important to remember that such an ROI needs to be realistic and to include all of the elements that account for a total cost of ownership. We have up to this point focused on the benefits of the business case, but when devising a realistic ROI for e-procurement initiatives, even for simple ORM projects, it is important to consider implementation costs that include

- Integration to your ERP and other back-end systems
- Both technical and process-focused user training
- Costs associated with helping suppliers to tie into the system

Outsourcing through ASPs may always be an option, but this type of approach has its drawbacks. Limited back-office systems integration and a dependency on an organization outside of your direct control are both serious issues. There have been innumerable cases of ASPs failing to deliver at agreed service levels, and, particularly if your project is focused on mission-critical MRO or direct materials, you will want to be certain of the cost/benefit ratio of an in-house versus ASP approach. Be certain when developing your strategy to consider all "total cost of ownership" variables.

Functionality

Any good e-procurement system will provide the basic catalog, ordering, and payment functionality, but it is important to remember that the success of ORM- and MRO-based requisitioning is dependent upon employees being able to easily complete transactions from their desktops. Therefore, ease of use is very important, especially in projects involving nonpurchasing employees. For the purchasing staff, it is also important that a system provides comprehensive, easy-to-use decision support and reporting tools.

It is always worthwhile, when preparing for a software vendor shortlist, to create a database of current procurement transactions, complete with paper forms used in the process, and to have the software vendor incorporate these directly into its solution presentation for your company. This "day-in-the-life" approach not only helps to contrast the differences between systems, but also forces the vendor to provide case-specific examples (as opposed to preorchestrated and often sweeping claims made in standard presentations) of how the software will deal with your organization's purchasing needs. Remember, too, of course, to make certain that the system can provide the level of data and access security that you need.

Integration and Interoperability

One of the most important criteria for selection, particularly if your organization is focusing on reducing the transaction costs (time, labor, errors, etc.) that come from manually rekeying data, is the system's ability to fully integrate both inward to your own ERP systems for automated approval and payment and outward to those of your suppliers. Links to in-house decision support systems will be key for either direct or indirect projects, and if the project involves direct goods, the system will need to interface directly with supply chain systems, as well as CRM systems and any e-commerce order fulfillment front end.

IMPLEMENTATION PHASE

As with major construction projects that always run long and over budget, underestimating implementation time for e-procurement projects is a chronic problem. One of the most important guiding principles to maintain is to always set proper expectations. It is to a large extent an effective early test of the proposing consultants to see exactly how they approach the issue. Ask them to help you to understand how much time you should allot for implementation, including system installation and training. Software vendors will often wave a dismissive hand and claim that implementation can be accomplished in as little as two months, but they may well be talking about a "slam-in-a-system" approach that will ultimately require a good deal more time, money, and rework to achieve the ROI that you are hoping for.

Try to judge how well your proposed supplier or consultant understands your business requirements. Do they focus on your specific business area, or do they specialize in certain commodity groups? Have them load several examples of your current data into the proposed system—an example PO or invoice—and have them walk you through a day-in-the-life scenario to see how well they know the procurement process and their own system's functionality. You may be surprised to find out just how inexperienced and unsure the consultants (who, after all, in this economic climate have probably been rushed through a certifying training course and dropped directly onto a project proposal) really are about the functionality of their systems.

It is important also to understand whether your proposed software vendor will implement the system themselves or whether they will have a VAR (value-added reseller) or service provider do it for them. If they are proposing a VAR, or for that matter an ASP, understand their approach to implementation, their previous record for similar implementations, and examine their financial standing. Many VARs, anxious to take advantage of the high margins, are rushing to call themselves ASPs these days, and if you do consider choosing that route, again, you will want to consider issues such as performance history, scalability, reliability, and penalty provision for violation of service level agreements.

Customer Support

In this same vein, and given the complexity and mission-critical nature of the software, it is important to understand the availability of technical support and the standards for service that the company has when resolving more difficult and time-consuming system problems. Consider, for example, the numbers of customers that the vendor currently has, its customer support infrastructure, and the nature of its service level agreements, support desk, and issue resolution offerings.

Future Viability of the Group

Finally, try to make a considered judgment on the mid-term viability of the software itself. This is not going to be easy to do, given the volatility of the marketplace, but try to develop an algorithm that gives value to a weighted scoring of key variables, such as

- Scalability
- Vision
- Development plans
- Vendor's history of adhering to announcement dates
- Future integration and/or operability plans
- Major changes to functionality that may make the vendor vulnerable to takeover or other risks

Size, financial strength, market position, and a stable management structure are all good indicators of future performance, but even these variables, as we have seen, cannot be guaranteed to give you an absolute assurance of future viability. In the end, you may be able to use the exercise only to identify and eliminate potentially dangerous liaisons with niche-platform providers, and will, like the rest of the business community, still be forced to make a decision based on functionality, service level histories, and total cost.

ENDNOTE

1. Reilly, B., "E-Procurement: A Blueprint for Revolution or Hype?," *Gartner Advisory, Strategic Analysis Report,* The Gartner Group, February 9, 2000, p. 15.

13 The Executive E-Procurement Strategy Workshop

Objective

There is nothing more important to a successful e-pro-curement intitiative than executive sponsorship. Com-pleting an executive strategy workshop can help to ensure that your organizational leaders understand the key fea-tures of an e-procurement strategy, and reach an early consensus on approach, sponsorship responsibilities, and on the need to take action.

■ The executive e-procurement strategy workshop should be attended by key organizational leaders, including company officers.

■ Use the workshop as an opportunity to educate the group on broad aspects of e-procurement.

■ Get the group to come to a consensus on key areas such as the case for action, guiding principles, project timescales, and who will be the program manager.

■ Capture all resolutions and decisions in real-time in order to create a "constitution" for the project.

As we have seen, in order to avoid the problems and pitfalls that so many organizations encounter with e-procurement projects, it is important to take the time with the executives to debate and reach agreement on e-procurement in the context of your overall business strategy—what it is, who it affects, why it is important, and what you should do as an organization to implement it.

As the first and most important step in your change management program, conduct a strategic alignment workshop with senior executives and important organizational leaders.

As the first and most important step in your change management program, conduct a strategic alignment workshop with senior executives and important organizational leaders at the beginning of any major e-procurement initiative to get consensus on the scope of the project, the case for action, the likely approach, and the necessary level of resources, time, and money.

Even if (especially if) such a gathering is likely to result in strong opinions being voiced and the project put at risk until agreement is reached, it is better to surface and resolve contentious issues at the beginning of the initiative than to have to fight those battles six months into the project plan, when there is much less flexibility of action.

The advantages of this type of workshop approach are twofold. First, it is a unique and logical forum for educating all the executives to the same level on e-procurement themes, allowing them an opportunity to thoroughly discuss and come to a consensus on crucial issues concerning the e-procurement initiative—dealing in a structured way with key issues, from business justification to project approach and staffing. Getting all your key organizational leaders to the same level of understanding and consensus at the beginning of the project is not only the first key step in project management, but a first crucial step in change management, as well.

Second, the ultimate output of the workshop becomes a foundation-planning document—essentially a "constitution"—which serves as the charter for the entire e-procurement initiative. This constitution is valuable not only in providing critical guidance to the project team, but also as a communication tool for the rest of the organization.

The executive e-procurement workshop should be held in a comfortable working area, usually off-site and away from distractions and interruptions, with plenty of whiteboard space and flip charts available. Your key organization leaders—usually between 10 and 12 people in all—should attend, including the Chief Executive, Chief Financial Officer, Director of MIS, Chief Operations Officer, Chief Procurement Officer, and other senior leaders who will be crucial to the project's success. The group should include representatives from key areas of the process, including central purchasing, accounting and finance, MIS, sales, and customer service. If yours is a manufacturing or distribution company considering a direct materials project, representatives from your supply chain—forecasting and planning, maintenance purchasing, replenishment, and supplier management—should attend as well.

You will also require an effective, independent facilitator and a "scribe" to take down information real-time on a laptop.

STEP ONE: DEFINING AND AGREEING ON FUNDAMENTALS

Because e-procurement means many things to many people, it is important to begin the strategic process by simply debating and coming to a consensus on the purpose and scope of the project. A few straightforward questions should be used to warm the group up:

- Why is this e-procurement project necessary?
- Why now?
- What are you hoping to achieve?
- What must you do to achieve it?
- How will you know when you have succeeded?
- What changes will be necessary?
- What needs to be done to ensure success?

Answers to those questions, as important as they are, may not be as intuitive as they first appear. It often helps, at the beginning of the strategic definition process, to examine the *case for action* first. Again, simple questions can prompt a serious discussion:

■ Why does the group believe that your organization should change your procurement process? Are they talking about ORM, MRO, or direct materials?

■ How do you know you must change, and what *benefits* are you hoping to gain?

  – Process efficiencies
  – Leverage
  – Compliance

■ Do you have any real figures yet on the cost or savings implications?

■ Can materials be easily divided into *categories,* such as strategic materials, materials that require a close vendor relationship, and commoditized or tactical products that can be bought more readily through exchanges or auctions?

■ Consider also how quickly you need to make any changes, and inversely, what happens if your organization decides to do nothing.

One important question is simply to ask yourselves how, as an executive team, you will know when you succeed with an e-procurement project. Invariably, this will initiate a discussion about what types of *performance indicators* will accurately demonstrate any improvements. It is a good time to ask how the procurement process is evaluated today, and how well that process is performing against current performance measures.

One of the most important discussions should center around what *guiding principles* will govern the initiative. For example, is the project about indirect or direct purchasing? Is outsourcing an option? How does the management team intend to deal with the issue of displaced employees—those workers in the current procurement process who deal in manual work that will be eliminated by the system? Will they be retrained and relocated? What will your policy be on releasing people? Do you plan to communicate openly and honestly with the employees? Do you plan to use the opportunity to restructure the entire process, or is this primarily a systems installation project?

Finally, if this is going to be an enterprise-wide initiative, it is worth thinking at the outset about representation from all the *key stakeholders* in the process. Do you have representatives from

- Procurement
- Accounting and finance
- Logistics, warehousing, and inventory management
- Manufacturing and production
- Information technology
- New product design
- Key vendors and partners

If not, it is probably worthwhile incorporating them into the project at the earliest possible moment, in order to avoid their missing out on early and valuable information and consensus building.

STEP TWO: EDUCATION ON E-PROCUREMENT

It is usually worthwhile to get someone from a local university, management consultancy, or IT industry analysis group to give a short explanatory lecture on e-procurement to your executive team—its history, the key issues, and broad scenarios that have been explored in this book. It can be particularly important to help them not only to understand the strategic nature of e-procurement, but also to understand the broad trends and rapid uptake of e-procurement solutions within the economy as a whole. This education session also tends to help broaden the procurement picture, placing the process much more in a strategic, rather than tactical, light.

STEP THREE: REVIEWING THE BUSINESS VISION

Before committing to an enterprise-wide e-procurement initiative, it is often worthwhile to consider first the way in which you anticipate your organization is moving strategically during the next one to three years. Depending on what business you are in, for example, you may be able to foresee dramatic changes to how you produce or sell your products or services. Those products and services themselves may be changing significantly. Will you be moving toward more online order fulfillment? Do you anticipate levels of growth or new geographical territories that might mean making greater demands of your suppliers or else shifting toward others? Are you in an industry that has begun to participate in vertical e-trading communities, which may force you to do the same?

Alternatively, ask yourself if there will be *changes in customer demands and expectations* in the next few years that would, in turn, change the way that you do business with your key suppliers. For example, will moving online mean a shift toward providing your customers with the possibility of customization or order tracking, which would, in turn, require a much tighter integration with the systems of your suppliers?

Are your *key suppliers beginning to change their expectations of you* in light of the e-procurement revolution? Many vendor groups are consolidating or collaborating in developing electronic trading communities, and may be trying to differentiate themselves significantly by changing their entire service offerings—focusing on managing a customer's inventory much more closely, monitoring and automatically refilling certain material groups, or overall becoming a much closer partner with their buyers. Will they expect you, as a client, to be moving toward electronic procurement capabilities?

It is sometimes worthwhile understanding, either through *benchmarking* or through a formal leading-practice study, what your competitors are planning on doing in these areas. You may well find that there are new opportunities in vertical exchanges or auctions that could provide significant benefit in purchasing high-volume materials. Often, if prearranged, a high-level benchmarking analysis can be provided during the education segment of the workshop to provide relevant industry-wide examples of costs and benefits.

STEP FOUR: UNDERSTAND THE PROCUREMENT BUSINESS CASE

Having already learned a little about e-procurement, it is helpful to have the executive team examine the procurement process end-to-end. For many executives—even in manufacturing—this may be the first time they have had the opportunity to discuss or understand efficiency and workflow problems; compliance issues; transaction costs; failures to adequately exert leverage; the amount of time spent by purchasing personnel in administrative, low-value work; strategic sourcing policies; and other issues. Typical questions might be

- What are the general purchasing rules?
- Are they consistent or do they vary widely between departments?
- Are they understood and adhered to by everyone?

Chances are, the answers to these types of questions will highlight the huge amount of potential savings to be made simply from focusing on applying leading practices (whether electronic or not) to the procurement process. These are the types of discussions that will open an executive's eyes to the potential value of an e-procurement initiative.

For ORM and MRO purchasing, also consider issues such as

- The amount of manual work, data redundancy, and rekeying that takes place daily
- Examples of long waits for approval and of high rates of checking and control (multiple stop, wait, approval points)
- Returns
- Extensive information exchange
- Maverick and off-contract buying
- Lack of strategic sourcing and discount leveraging

For direct materials purchasing, consider

- Costs of safety stock and excessive inventory buffers
- Interruptions on manufacturing/shop floor due to lack of maintenance or direct materials (MRO)
- Returns or no shows
- Failures to adhere to pricing policies and negotiated discounts
- Frustrations with your inability to develop a consistent and enforceable plan for strategic sourcing

Consider how major changes in the procurement process will affect the organization. Review the *current information technology systems* and consider how they would interface with an e-procurement system.

- Are there separate systems for accounting, requisitioning, receiving, central purchasing, and payment?
- Are there disparate systems used in different departments?

- What are your current capabilities with regard to EDI and XML?

- Do all employees who might need to make purchases have access to a computer?

Review the staff numbers and various skills associated with the upkeep of these various systems. Are there other major IT initiatives currently underway? Is part of the goal of the project to simply consolidate and rationalize the many different systems and practices that exist throughout the firm?

Remember, too, that much of the success of any e-procurement initiative is dependent upon a widespread change in employee buying behavior. Ask yourselves if your organization has a maverick buying culture. Are your purchasing specialists frustrated with having to complete insignificant but time-consuming administrative duties while key strategic sourcing and vendor relationship management duties are left uncompleted?

These types of issues overlap into the realm of change management and should prompt executives to appreciate some of the key personnel issues related to an e-procurement project.

STEP FIVE: DEVELOPING SCENARIOS

By this time in the workshop, many of the group will have already put forward suggestions for change, and it is a good time to begin building high-level consensus around these proposals. Begin by drawing out several possible scenarios. These might be, for example,

- Focusing on ORM and MRO with desktop requisitioning

- Combining in-house systems with partial ASP outsourcing for catalog maintenance

- Concentrating on direct procurement first, with full ERP integration

- Dividing commodities into strategic and tactical; beginning with tactical first

- Investigating auctions and exchanges for commodity purchasing and providing central purchasing specialists with portal subscriptions

With further discussion and refinement, these scenarios will begin to take logical shape and the group will be in a position to see exactly what information is still required before all of the pros and cons of each scenario can be appreciated and a decision on the way forward reached. Tying each scenario back to the group's original guiding principles will help to quickly validate or bring into question each broad proposal.

One important question that should be put forward at this time is, What more, exactly, does the group need to know before any decision on moving ahead can be agreed upon? Although collecting the information necessary for this type of business case confirmation should take place during the analysis and design phases of the project, it is important that a specific set of tasks be agreed upon by the group, which will provide the necessary information to make a decision by an agreed-upon time.

STEP SIX: PROJECT READINESS REVIEW

Based on the discussions and scenarios put forward, it is worthwhile to set preliminary milestones for the project. There are some critical issues to be addressed. What are the recommended timescales for the project? What tentative dates should be set for key milestones, such as

- The end of the data collection, verification, and planning phase
- Systems selection
- Systems implementation
- Legacy systems integration
- Supplier systems integration
- Transition and training for employees
- Realization of ROI

Before the executive group breaks up, there are several important issues that need to be addressed regarding the readiness of the organization to take on the proposed project. It can help to review the results of any major ERP or business process reengineering (BPR) initiatives that the organization has done in the past that had a similar enterprise-wide effect. Were there cultural or organizational issues that disrupted or mitigated the success of these past initiatives? If so, what does the executive group need to do this time in order to avoid such disruption?

It is worthwhile polling the executive group to see if they believe the organization is ready to undertake an e-procurement project such as the one proposed in the scenarios. Do they believe they have a strong case for action? Does the organization have the committed leadership, skills, and resources necessary to successfully execute a major e-procurement effort? What problems do they anticipate, and what does the executive group need to do to overcome those problems?

Possibly the most important thing of all, if you decide to move forward with an e-procurement project, is to make certain to discuss and get agreement on the need for a strong program manager who will be responsible for the overall success of the project. Discuss also the probable project structure and the need for the executives to play a continuing active role in the sponsorship and communication portions of the initiative. All of these activities are related to a broad program of change management, which increasingly needs to be formalized and incorporated into the project structure.

Creating an Effective Plan of Change Management

Initiatives that have an IT solution as their core often fail to appreciate the need for an integrated program of change management. But change management should never be seen as a "bolt-on" with important enterprise-wide projects:

■ People issues are the primary obstacle to implementing large-scale projects, and are rated higher among companies complaining of failed initiatives than technology and process issues combined.

■ The best way to ensure that changes to process and work activities really occur is to build change management into the project structure from the outset.

■ The best way to continue to maintain a high level of executive sponsorship is to continue to engage those executives throughout the project.

■ The program manager serves as the single, most knowledgeable liaison between the executives and teams.

I t is surprising that despite the fact that an era of some near-disaster ERP implementations is just **"I'm all for progress," explained Mark Twain. "It's change I don't like."**[1] winding down, many executives still often fail to ensure that key project change management tasks are incorporated in the overall e-business initiative.

Part of the reason for this, I have found from my own experience, is that "change management" is a phrase that rings alarm bells with many of the uninitiated. In part, this is the fault of the very soft, "behaviorist" side of change management consulting, whose proponents, like psychoanalysts, have promised much but actually delivered very little true and lasting business benefit to clients. I have witnessed too many skeptical executives roll their eyes and exclaim, "We don't want any of that soft stuff." With a poor record of success in "transforming" company cultures and teaching organizational leaders how to be entrepreneurial, these efforts (unfairly still grouped under the heading of change management) have produced a backlash among the many disillusioned clients.

Yet key elements of change management—strong project management and employee communications plans; redesign of workflow, positions, and responsibilities; restructuring of reporting lines and incentive programs; development of technical and process training regimes; and implementation of a program for displaced staff—are neither soft nor dispensable.

In fact, a survey by Benchmarking Partners of 62 Fortune 500 companies implementing ERP found that people issues were the primary obstacle to implementing ERP and rated higher than both technology and process issues combined.[2] It was true of ERP, but it is even more important with e-procurement because, ultimately, the success of any initiative will be dependent upon broadly changing buyer behavior among your purchasing staff and employees.

As we have seen, there are several predictable areas where enterprise-wide e-procurement initiatives go wrong. These include:

- The nonpurchasing departmental executives and company officers see the project only as a large investment, exclusively purchasing and IT-based, with little or no benefit to their respective operational areas.

- If the e-procurement project is not seen by the executives as being strategic to the firm, and if the project lacks overall executive endorsement, there is a risk that the solution will be implemented on a piecemeal basis, reflecting traditional functional or departmental silos and traditional ways of working.

- Workflow and positions change planning is not considered until after technical systems implementation, which delays real business results.

- Lack of emphasis on communications (up or down) in the organization means there is little understanding of what the e-procurement project is intended to achieve, how employees will be affected, and how the project will benefit the company as a whole.

By contrast, those projects that have gone well have usually had common characteristics:

- Key executives understand and agree on the goals, approach, and timing of the project.

- E-procurement is planned and managed as a single, company-wide initiative (even if implemented in smaller pilot projects).

- The project is coordinated and managed through a strong, participative project management office that provides structure, clarity, integration and direction.

- The company takes the opportunity of implementing e-procurement to clean up purchasing work processes and techniques.

- Implications on changes to process and work activities are formally captured through an implications analysis, and change is formally managed through a change transition plan.

- Enthusiasm is created and resistance reduced through a comprehensive, executive-led communications program.

One of the most important lessons learned in these types of projects is to make certain that change management is not simply a "bolt-on" to a technical project. The best way to ensure that changes to process and work activities really do occur is to build change management directly into the project structure from the outset, and that can best be accomplished by structuring the project so it reflects the emphasis on business transformation, not just systems implementation.

Making that program of change management integral to the initiative can be done in two ways. The first is to make certain that the project is structured and staffed in a way that ensures that the necessary resources and skills are available and provided with the authority and support necessary to be successful. The second is to develop an integral plan for change management that incorporates several key areas that are far too often omitted with an initiative that has technology as its core solution. Let's first deal with the approach to project structure and staffing.

PROJECT STRUCTURE AND STAFFING

The Executive Steering Committee

As we have said before, a critical first step in a change management process is enlisting executive support and consensus. The best way to continue to maintain that level of sponsorship is to continue to engage those executives throughout the project by having them sit as a steering committee. For a time out of favor, placing a steering committee in charge is worth a word of caution, because as any of us who has either sat on a steering committee or worked with one in the past knows, there can be a tendency for the group to micromanage and second guess the project team, in ways that are not always best for the project. Nonetheless, executive understanding and sponsorship is too critical to have with an e-procurement initiative to allow the project to move ahead without direct executive participation.

In the end, the key to finding a balance between sponsorship and domination is usually dependent upon the personality and abilities of the program manager/project champion. She or he will ultimately need the political tact, the technical knowledge, and the respect of the leadership community to be able to continue to keep the executive officers informed and involved, without allowing them to choose the all-too-easy option of project by dictate.

E-Procurement Program Manager

E-procurement projects for indirect goods can be difficult, but are mainly straightforward in their goals and design. Many hundreds of companies have already shifted their indirect purchasing online, and therefore there is ample evidence of what works and what doesn't when it comes to a project approach. Direct is infinitely more complex and difficult, but many of the same principles and structures apply. In either case, there are a number of broad activity categories that need to be completed by someone—either from within the organization or from the software or consultancy world—in order for the project to be successful. These include

- Soliciting and guaranteeing the necessary levels of sponsorship from both company leaders and the supplier community
- Day-to-day project management
- Development and execution of the communications plan
- Completing the implications analysis on changes to people's work activities and the process, and developing a transition plan for changes to employees' jobs
- Both process and technical education and training
- Technical design and implementation of the software
- Technical design and implementation of the supporting IT systems, including integration and communications issues
- Benefits tracking

The responsibility for overseeing these various tasks will be different with each project, but it is important to recognize that someone needs to be charged with the successful completion of each of these broad activity areas, and clarity around that responsibility is essential to success.

As a deputy to the chief executive (or possibly to the chief procurement officer, in larger companies), the e-procurement program manager directs the entire project and has overall responsibility for making certain that each of the above areas is accomplished successfully. Constantly reinforcing the coordinated, enterprise-wide project viewpoint, the program manager provides high-level day-to-day project management, ensures consistency of approach and adherence to project guidelines and milestones, and serves as the highest level liaison for resolving issues with senior management that arise during the project. That means that he or she is continuously communicating with the executive steering committee, educating and updating the executive sponsors on project process, and facilitating executive resolution of major project issues as they arise. The program manager serves as the single, most knowledgeable liaison between the executives and the teams and is essentially the project "brain trust," single point of contact, spokesperson, and owner of project success.

Technical Program Director

Reporting directly to the program manager, the e-procurement technical program director is responsible for

- Design and implementation of the software solution
- Design and implementation of the supporting hardware, communications interfaces, data migration, and systems integration
- Technical end-user training and help desk setup

The technical director therefore oversees the entire investment in technical infrastructure and should be both a skilled MIS practitioner and an experienced IT project manager. He or she will need to have a good understanding of the procurement process and of various applications and how they interact. As the central point of contact with software vendors, the technical program director will require an understanding of broader business goals and the presence to resist the temptation to "slam in a system" at the expense of overall business benefits.

Nontechnical Program Director

The nontechnical program director is responsible for all non-IT aspects of the e-procurement project. This broadly encompasses three main categories: project risk and change management, business process and job role analysis and change, and business case management.

The nontechnical program director also works closely with the program manager and the executive sponsors on the steering committee to help ensure strong and visible executive sponsorship, and is ultimately responsible for creating and overseeing the delivery of the employee communications program. He or she also oversees project "health" and identifies—and is responsible for—resolving any personal or political issues that arise that might compromise the success of the project. This role also is responsible for deriving and documenting the changes to workflow and positions brought about by the new process and system (the implications analysis) and for assisting departmental leaders and Human Resources in creating a transition plan for helping employees with education and training on nontechnical (process and activity changes) issues. Finally, he or she is responsible for applying the "performance indicators" agreed upon by the executive and planning teams, and for building the business case and ROI over the course of the project.

Far too often, organizations assume that anyone dealing in people or position changes should be from human resources, but that is almost never the case. Usually a respected leader who is knowledgeable about the procurement process, whoever is appointed to this critical role needs to have the political presence, organizational familiarity, and personal tact to manage the most difficult half of the project—ensuring that the business actually derives a benefit from the new systems. Those qualities usually are found in long-serving organizational mid- to high-level managers who understand how procurement is done, can appreciate the need for change, are known and respected broadly, and have a healthy and engaging relationship with senior executives (Figure 14.1).

THE CORE TEAM

The core team should be made up of six to eight representatives from the key cross-functional areas of the procurement process. For ORM projects, that means requisitioning, supplier management, central purchasing, accounting and finance, MIS, and receiving. For indirect projects, a much broader input will be needed, including representatives from inventory management, new product design, forecasting and planning, manufacturing, logistics, and the key supplier community. As process experts, these representatives should thoroughly understand their own functional areas, and even better, the broad procurement process as a whole. Willing to become advocates of the new process and system, they also need to be recognized leaders in their areas, able to persuade their colleagues of the business case and to act as an "ambassador" for the project. Unfortunately, these are the same people who tend to be invaluable to a company on a day-to-day basis, but with strong management endorsement, it should be possible to adjust schedules to ensure that these key experts help design the new approach.

Occasionally, because of the issue of job changes, a representative from human resources is invited onto the team, either as a full-time or part-time member. This has its merits, particularly if the organization is likely to need to negotiate changes in union-agreed roles or levels. However, it is too often assumed that the representative from the human resources department has a broad background

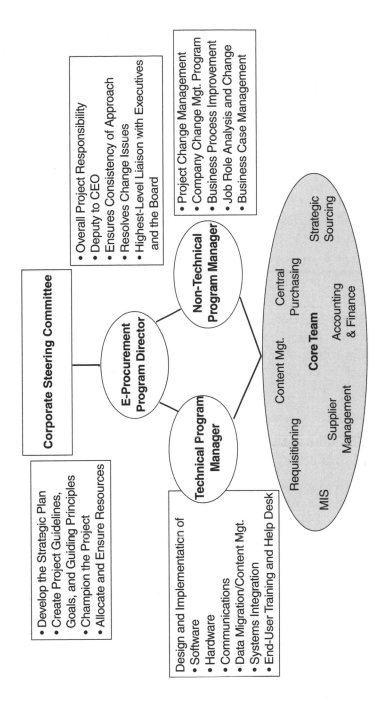

Figure 14.1 Project structure, roles, and responsibilities for an e-procurement initiative.

in all types of people management issues—including change management experience, organizational alignment, and skills assessment. That may or may not be the case, but it is important that the assumption is not automatically made, and that most of the responsibility for change management remain with the nontechnical program manager and his or her assistants.

The core team will usually be augmented by experts from a management consultancy or from the software provider or VAR, depending on the phase of the project. It is important, however, that this core group of employees sees the project as their responsibility and that they take a lead in extracting best practices from the consultants and software specialists, rather than passively seeing their role as merely explaining the current state to outsiders (consultants), who will then create the future direction for their company.

Subject Matter Experts and Supplier Representatives

Not only will you want various subject matter experts on, or at least available to, the core team, but it is often a good idea to also find the worst maverick-buying offenders and have them provide input as to why non-contract purchasing has been necessary in the past. It is also, of course, very valuable to get input from some of your most important or most progressive suppliers, concerning the vendor point of view.

CREATING A BUSINESS CHANGE IMPLEMENTATION PLAN

A good project plan for any enterprise-wide e-procurement initiative should always include a specific plan for enterprise-wide change transition. There are many variations, but whichever approach you decide to take, I have found that the approach should adhere to two guiding principles. First, change management should be integrally intertwined with the project approach itself, not seen as a separate or parallel program run by organizational or behavioral specialists. Second, the plan should be organized at a level that is comparable to that of the technical design and implementation plan, with key activities, milestones, and deliverables. *A business change transition plan should be of as much interest—if not more interest—to the executive steering committee as the technical implementation plan.* The best business change plans that I have encountered usually address, in one way or another, six broad categories:

1. **Communications.** As we have said before, an open and consistent communication plan, delivered at both the executive and operational levels, is crucial to ensuring buy-in for the project from the organization as a whole. This communication plan should begin with the output from the executive e-procurement workshop, and should be structured around key themes such as

   a. What is happening
   b. Why it is happening
   c. How it will affect employees
   d. When it will happen
   e. What employees need to do
   f. How employees will be provided further information and updates
   g. How the company will know when it is successful

   The key, of course, is to get the right message in the right format to the right people at the right time. Admittedly, for some, such a standardized and preplanned approach to communication hints of manipulation, but there need not be anything underhanded about the message simply because employees receive consistent information. Because so many of us have lived through many large projects in the past that incorporated a solid approach to communications, it may seem to go without saying, but an effective communications plan is absolutely critical to the success of the project.

2. **Project Risk Management.** This area encompasses many of the project-related activities normally associated with change management, including developing a strong, company-wide communications plan, scheduling one-on-one interviews between the program manager, the nontechnical program manager, and various executives or organizational leaders, identifying and resolving personal conflicts between members of the project team, identifying issues—a recalcitrant or unsupportive executive, union resistance, lack of representation in the project from a key group—that might put the success of the project at risk. Strategies to limit these types of risk may include communication-related activities such as employee forums, an e-procurement road show, or even team training or "out-of-the-box thinking" events.

3. **Positions and Structure.** There will be many key structural changes that will occur to the procurement process as the company shifts from manual to electronic and from centralized to employee-initiated purchasing. Most importantly, this area includes making certain that the implications analysis is completed in conjunction with the systems design, and identifying changes to the process and job positions of current procurement staff. It also involves

   a. Prototyping new job descriptions
   b. Identifying new skill level requirements
   c. Conducting a skills inventory of current staff
   d. Defining the staffing redeployment plan

4. **Training and Development.** As with all employee desktop systems, at least with indirect materials purchasing, it will be necessary to provide training to the employee end users on the software and approach to desktop requisitioning. Such training courses are often provided by the software vendor, but will need to be coordinated and, at times, modified to reflect your company's purchasing policies. For those employees whose jobs are displaced by the system, it will be necessary to create new training courses that will help them to update their skills and cope with the change.

5. **Performance Management.** Identifying and beginning to record meaningful and accurate performance measures is critical to the success of an e-procurement initiative. Not only do these figures become part of the business justification process, but in the future will be used to help build an accurate, real-time view of both supplier and procurement process performance.

6. **Rewards and Recognition.** Finally, remembering that the effectiveness of desktop requisitioning comes in large part from adherence to rules concerning standardized buying policies, it is often important to identify specific guidelines for purchasing goods and to create specific incentives for adhering to them.

ENDNOTES

1. Quotation attributed to Mark Twain.
2. Corini, John, "Integrating e-Procurement and Strategic Sourcing," *Supply Chain Management Review,* March 2000, p. 7.

INDEX

Page numbers in italics refer to illustrations.

e-procurement strategy workshop (*continued*)
   fundamentals of, 178–80
   issues, 181–83
   scenarios, 183–84
   steps of, 178–85
EAI (Enterprise Application Integration), 123
EAM (Enterprise Asset Management), 94
eBay, 82
eBreviate.com, 91
eCO Framework X, 105
Economist, The, 6
EDI (Electronic Data Interchange) systems, 12, 30
   explanation of, 37, 61–62
   transactions, 101–3
EDS, 105
education, 180, 196
EFDEX, 98
electronic auctions, 8–9, 64, 88–93
   advantages of, 89, 92, 129
   case study, 90
   drawbacks of, 92–93
   explanation of, 88–89
   fees for, 89
   indirect materials and, 82
   reverse auctions, 91
   vendors and, 125
electronic catalogs
   access to, 86
   buyer-managed, 79
   creation of, 62
   explanation of, 32–33, 48–49
   maintaining, 76
Electronic Data Interchange (EDI) systems, 12, 30
   explanation of, 37, 61–62
   transactions, 101–3
electronic payments, 71–72
electronic signature, 135–36
electronic trading communities, 64, 66–67, 86.
   See also trading hubs
   benefits of, 74
   growth of, 80–82
   participants in, 84
employee participation, 167–68, 170–72
encryption issues, 134–37
Enterprise Application Integration (EAI), 123
Enterprise Asset Management (EAM), 94
Enterprise Resource Planning (ERP) suppliers, 67–69
Enterprise Resource Planning (ERP) systems, 10, 12, 15
   benefits of, 32, 33
   e-procurement support, 50, 67–68, 132–33
   government agencies and, 115
   importance of, 39

initial use of, 39–41
materials management, 14, 123
obstacles to implementing, 187
purchasing processes and, 36, 77–78
enterprise suites, 65–66. *See also* third-party software
   costs of, 133–34
   examples of, 112–13, 124
enterprise-wide project, 142–44, 148–50, *162*
ERP (Enterprise Resource Planning) suppliers, 67–69
ERP (Enterprise Resource Planning) systems, 10, 12, 15
   benefits of, 32, 33
   e-procurement support, 50, 67–68, 132–33
   government agencies and, 115
   importance of, 39
   initial use of, 39–41
   materials management, 14, 123
   obstacles to implementing, 187
   purchasing processes and, 36, 77–78
Essential Markets.com, 94
Etoys, 4
EU (European Union), 109, 113–14
EUR, 113
Europe, 12–13
European Union (EU), 109, 113–14
exchange companies, 84–88
   failure of, 97–98
executive workshop, 176–85. *See also* e-procurement strategy workshop
Exosta, 116
experts on procurement process, 192–94
extended enterprise, 38–39, 41
Extensible Markup Language (XML). *See* XML (Extensible Markup Language)
Extricity, 65, 69

F
Federal Express, 11, 105
Fedmarket.com, 111
Ford, 9, 84, 105
Forrester Research, 12
Free Trade Zone, 89
FreeMarkets Inc., 91
FreeMarkets.com, 92
frpMarket.com, 91
fulfillment
   automation of, 123
   components of, *10*
   e-procurement and, 41, 64
   efficiency of, 10–11
   management of, 49
fundamentals of e-procurement strategy, 178–80

ROI (*continued*)
  requisitioning software and, 79
  skepticism and, 147
  subscription services and, 134
  transaction costs and, 18
Rooster.com, 85
RosettaNet, 103, 105

S

Sabre Reservation, 122
Safeway, 84
sales, expanding, 130
Samsung, 84
SAP
  e-procurement and, 123
  platform integration, 67, 106, 115
  third-party software and, 69
SAP R/3, 52
SAPMarkets, 71
SAS Institute, 55
SAS Solution's Supplier Relationship
  Management System, 32
scenarios, developing, 183–84
SciQuest, 89
Sears, 84
secure certificates, 135
secure file transfers, 103
security issues, 14, 134–37
self-service procurement system, 51, 59
sell-side one-to-many model, 75–77, *76*
sensitive procurement transactions, 136
SGML (Standard Generalized Markup
  Language), 102
Shell, 84
Shepherd, Jim, 139
shipping and receiving, 38. *See also* fulfillment
"Shocking Economic Effect of B2B, The," 6
shopping malls, 64, 75–77
Simap system, 113
single-solution suppliers, 97–98, 122–25
smart cards, 135
Smartmission, 114
Smith, Jim, 57
SmithKline Beecham, 91, 92
Society for Worldwide Interbank Financial
  Telecommunications (SWIFT), 103
software specialists, 65–71, *70*
  benefits of, 152–53
  platform integration, 123–24
software suites. *See* enterprise suites; third-
  party software
staff responsibility, 170–72, 190
staffing changes, 147, 189–92, 196
stakeholders, 180
Standard Generalized Markup Language
  (SGML), 102

storefront models, 75–77
strategic planning, value of, 163–64
strategic sourcing, 55–59, 66
  explanation of, 96–97
  understanding, 181–83
  vendors and, 125, 183
structuring e-procurement projects, 160–75.
  See also e-procurement project
subscription services, 134
Sun Microsystem/Netscape, 65, 103
supplier-buyer relationships, 134–37, 166–67,
  181, 183
Supplier Market.com, 65
SupplierMarket.com, 86, 90, 91
suppliers. *See also* vendors
  participation of, 151–52
  relationships, 134–37, 166–67, 181, 183
  support from, 151–52, 169
supply chain materials, 13
supply chain procurement, 13, 14
  automation of, 36–39, 67–69
supply chain relationships, 12, 15
supply chain software, 32, 124. *See also*
  enterprise suites; vendors
supply chain systems, 10–11, 123–26
SWIFT (Society for Worldwide Interbank
  Financial Telecommunications), 103
SynQuest, 68
system selection, 172–74
system-to-system integration issues, 131–33,
  150–51

T

Talsi, Mikko, 150
TanData Corp, 66
Target, 84
team-based purchasing, 59
team members, 171–72, 192–94
technical program director, 191
technology curve, *7*
technology, expansion of, *7*
Tesco, 84
Texas Instruments, 11
third-party hosts, 63–66, 93, *94*
  future of, 119–20
third-party software, 65–66. *See also*
  connectors; enterprise suites
  competition, *70*
  connectivity and, 69, 71
  platform integration, 96, 124
3M Corporation, 8, 34
tier-one vendors, 9, 12
total procurement information systems, 32
TPN Marketplace, 34
TPN Register, 34
tracking capabilities, 38, 50

tracking costs, 19, 33
Tradeair, 117
TRADEC.com e-procurement system, 56–57
TradeMatrix, 67, 124
TradeMatrix Procurement Services, 68
Tradeum, 124
trading communities. *See* electronic trading
    communities; trading hubs
trading hubs, 64. *See also* electronic trading
    communities
    fees for, 88, 134
    platform integration, 86, 95–96
    vendor rationalization, 125
training, 180, 196
transactions, 25–26
    cost savings, 16–19, 25–26, 101–3, 145–47
    fees for, 88
    in purchasing, 30–32, 123, 131
    security of, 135–37
    simplification of, 86
    time required, 35
Trilogy, 65
Trilogy Software, 133

U

U. S. Department of Defense, 115, 116, 136
U. S. Department of the Treasury, 135
United Kingdom, 13, 141
United Technologies, 11, 92, 117
UPS, 66
Usinternetworking, 134

V

value-added reseller (VAR), 174, 194
value-added services, 125–26
Van Keulen, Kathy, 34
VAR (value-added reseller), 174, 194
VEBA Electronics, 56
Vendor-Managed Inventory (VMI), 12
vendors. *See also* suppliers
    inventory, 146
    online catalogs, 32–33
    participation, 151–52
    rationalization, 55, 58, 125
    relationships, 134–37, 166–67, 181, 183
    software specialists, 65–71, *70*
    support from, 151–52, 169
    tier-one, 9, 12
Ventro, 98, 124

vertical e-markets, 76, 82–85
    advantages of, 85
    examples of, 82–83
    explanation of, 82–83
    forecasts by industry, *83*
    integration of, 120–22, 124
    shakeouts, 98
VerticalNet, 111, 124
Visa USA, 71
Visio, 79
VMI (Vendor-Managed Inventory), 12
Volpe Brown Whelan & Company, 82

W

W. W. Grainger
    case study, 87
    e-procurement, 86, 130
    procurement spending, 12, 13, 15
    return on investment (ROI), 18
Wall Street Journal, 17
Web-based procurement, 74–99
Web-based technology, 10
Web sites, 4, 41
WebMethods, 69, 124
WebSphere Commerce, 67, 124
Weyerhauser, 85
white collar ORM, 26–27. *See also* ORM
    (Operating Resource Management)
Williams, Lisa, 26
Wood River Technologies, 111
workshops, 163–64, 167–68, 176–85. *See also*
    e-procurement strategy workshop
World Wide Web, 7
WorldWide Retail Exchange, 84

X

xCBL (XML Common Business Library), 103,
    105
XML (Extensible Markup Language), 100–106
    connectivity and, 69, 71, 119, 123
    example of, *104*
    explanation of, 100, 102–3
    formats, 77, 94
    product suite, 124
XML Interoperability Bus Architecture, 105
XML.cor, 105

Y

Yankee Group, 26

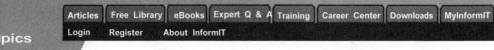